"Nicholas Wolterstorff here gives us a *true* liturgical theology — not a theology about liturgy but, rather, the explicit and implicit theology in the actions and order of worship. The ripple effects are profound, implicating understandings of God, persons, time, prayer, lament, and much more. There is little doubt that this book will be a landmark in the terrain of liturgical theology."

— LEANNE VAN DYK
Western Theological Seminary

"A good many books on liturgical theology discuss everything under the sun other than actual liturgies themselves. In this timely study Wolterstorff brings his sharp philosophical and theological mind to bear on specific liturgical texts and explores how the church, in enacting the liturgy, hands on its implicit understanding of God. This work will be a crucial text for any serious study of liturgical theology."

— BRYAN SPINKS
Yale Divinity School

The Lord said, "I have heard the cry of my people."

adapted from Exodus 3:7

The Kantzer Lectures in Revealed Theology

Sponsored by the
Carl F. H. Henry Center for Theological Understanding,
Trinity Evangelical Divinity School

SERIES EDITORS

Thomas H. McCall • Douglas A. Sweeney • Kevin J. Vanhoozer

PUBLISHED

The Election of Grace: A Riddle without a Resolution?
Stephen N. Williams

The God We Worship: An Exploration of Liturgical Theology
Nicholas Wolterstorff

The God We Worship

An Exploration of Liturgical Theology

Nicholas Wolterstorff

WILLIAM B. EERDMANS PUBLISHING COMPANY
GRAND RAPIDS, MICHIGAN / CAMBRIDGE, U.K.

Published 2015 by
Wm. B. Eerdmans Publishing Co.
2140 Oak Industrial Drive N.E., Grand Rapids, Michigan 49505 /
P.O. Box 163, Cambridge CB3 9PU U.K.

Printed in the United States of America

21 20 19 18 17 16 15   7 6 5 4 3 2 1

Library of Congress Cataloging-in-Publication Data

Wolterstorff, Nicholas.
The God we worship: an exploration of liturgical theology /
Nicholas Wolterstorff.
        pages   cm
ISBN 978-0-8028-7249-4 (pbk.: alk. paper)
1. God (Christianity) — Worship and love.   I. Title.

BV4817.W65   2015
231 — dc23
                            2014042013

www.eerdmans.com

Contents

Series Foreword

The Kantzer Lectures in Revealed Theology are intended to be the evangelical equivalent of the celebrated Gifford Lectures in natural theology.

The Gifford Lectures were established in 1885 by a generous provision in Adam Lord Gifford's will, in which he stipulated that the lectures be held alternately at each of the four universities of Scotland.

Since their inception, the Gifford Lectures have provided a quasi-institutional, university-based framework for seeking knowledge of God on the basis of science, philosophy, and nature. Taken as a whole, the Gifford Lectures constitute a record of the most important intellectual trends of the twentieth century. However, though Lord Gifford expressed a desire that the lecturers be "sincere lovers of and earnest inquirers after truth," he also stipulated that they treat their subject "as a strictly natural science, . . . that of infinite Being, without reference to or reliance upon any supposed special exceptional or so-called miraculous revelation."

While agreeing with Lord Gifford's premise that all people should benefit from the knowledge of God that "lies at the root of well-being," the Kantzer Lectures begin where the Gifford Lectures leave off: with a sustained focus on the knowledge of God located in God's Word, on the self-presentation of the triune God in the history of redemption, and on its scriptural attestation that culminates in the person and history of Jesus Christ.

It is most appropriate that these lectures in revealed theology take their name from the late Kenneth S. Kantzer (1917-2002). Dr. Kantzer's career spanned the course of the resurgence of North American evangelicalism and was one of the factors that spurred it on. Dr. Kantzer served as professor of biblical and systematic theology at Wheaton College for seventeen years, as Dean of Trinity Evangelical Divinity School for fifteen more, and as editor-in-chief of *Christianity Today.* In 1984 he returned to Trinity, where he eventually became the first director of a Ph.D. program in theological studies. In each of these roles, he was motivated by a heartfelt desire that theology be of service to the church: "Scripture was given to the church, and theology is a necessary work of the church, by the church, in the church, and for the church."

Dr. Kantzer's most important legacy was not a monetary bequest but a divinity school: Trinity Evangelical Divinity School. It was his vision to combine centrist evangelical theological convictions with a commitment to academic excellence. His concern was to help evangelicals major in the majors rather than the minors. In this sense, he was the epitome of the "catholic evangelical." ("The role of church tradition," he once wrote, "is like that of an elder brother in the faith.") He was a model of graciousness who would criticize only after listening charitably. ("Differences are not necessarily contradictions.") He was one of the first evangelicals, for example, to go to Basel and learn from Karl Barth. He completed his Ph.D. at Harvard University, where he wrote a dissertation focused on the knowledge of God in the theology of John Calvin. It is therefore fitting that the lectures that bear his name be located at the institution into which he poured not only the best years of his life, but also his passion, energy, and wisdom.

The Kantzer Lectures speak to what the sociologist Alan Wolfe describes in his book *The Transformation of American Religion* as the "strange disappearance of doctrine in the church." All too often, biblical and theological doctrines have been displaced, discarded, or forgotten in favor of therapeutic, relational, or managerial knowledge drawn less from the canonical Scriptures than from the canon of contemporary popular culture.

The Kantzer Lectures address the crisis of theology in the church. In particular, they confront the powerful, and not entirely unwarranted, prejudice that theology is irrelevant and unrelated to real life. They do this by showing how the knowledge of God derived from revealed theology is indeed practical.

The special focus of the Kantzer Lectures is on the development of doctrine from Scripture and on the ways in which doctrine gives rise to the *lived* knowledge of God. Given the increasingly complex world in which the church now lives, there is nothing more practical, yet elusive, than Christian wisdom. Hence the aim of the lectures is not to add to the church's stock of information — who, what, where — but rather to the church's wisdom and understanding, and hence to the church's witness and well-being. Revealed theology deals not with arcane or obsolete knowledge; theology is no trivial pursuit. On the contrary, as both Calvin and Kantzer insist, the knowledge of God is intrinsically linked with self-knowledge and with knowing how to live well to God's glory.

If evangelical theology has a constructive contribution to make to the contemporary church, it is its passion to root Christian thinking and living in the realities of the gospel of Jesus Christ. To focus on revealed theology is not to bury our heads in ancient Palestinian sand, however, but rather to approach our era's most pressing challenges with the resources of Trinitarian faith. The Kantzer Lectures provide a platform for this kind of Christian thinking, featuring prominent theologians committed to the project of faith seeking understanding, and to making this understanding practical. Hence the remit of the Kantzer Lectures in Revealed Theology: get wisdom; get understanding; get the mind of Christ.

THOMAS H. McCALL
DOUGLAS A. SWEENEY
KEVIN J. VANHOOZER

Acknowledgments

In the fall of 2013 I delivered the Kantzer Lectures in Revealed Theology at Trinity Evangelical Divinity School in Deerfield, Illinois. This essay is a revision of the text of those lectures. I thank Trinity for the honor of being invited to give the lectures, for the extraordinary hospitality I enjoyed while I was on the campus, and for the astute and helpful comments that students and professors made in the question period after each lecture. I also thank a group of students at the University of Virginia, organized by Matthew Puffer, for reading and offering me helpful comments on an early draft of the lectures; and Terence Cuneo, for likewise reading and commenting on a version of these lectures.

CHAPTER ONE

The Project: Liturgical Theology

Theology comes in many different configurations. In his *Summa Theologiae* Aquinas structured theology to fit what he regarded as the requirements for something's being a science — in Latin, *scientia*. He began with a proof of the existence of the object of this particular *scientia,* namely, God. Reality is so structured, Aquinas argued, that there must be something that is the unconditioned condition of all that is not identical with itself; this we all call "God," he says. The fact that God is the unconditioned condition of all that is not identical with God implies, so Aquinas argued in a long chain of deductions, that God is simple, perfect, good, infinite, immutable, eternal, and so forth.

The theology that Calvin developed in the *Institutes* had a very different configuration. It presented a way of interpreting Scripture that was aimed at cultivating in readers what Calvin called "piety" — piety being understood as "that reverence joined with love of God which the knowledge of [God's] benefits induces" (*Institutes* I.ii.1).[1] Whereas the doctrine of divine simplicity had looming importance in the configuration that Aquinas gave to theology, it had none at all in Calvin's configuration.

A good deal of theology is what one might call *conciliar* or *creedal* theology; it takes as its basic subject matter doctrines debated and decided in the early ecumenical councils and summarized in the Nicene and Apostles' creeds, the doctrines of Trinity and Incarnation being foremost among those. Other theology is *confessional* theology; it takes as its basic

---

1. The translation of the *Institutes* that I will be using is that by Ford Lewis Battles (Philadelphia: Westminster Press, 1960). The passage quoted is on p. 41.

1

subject matter doctrines formulated in one or another of the Reformation confessions, the doctrines of election and justification prominent among those. And over the centuries a great deal of theology, with epistemological concerns in mind, has employed revelation as its overarching category.

Schleiermacher's theology in *The Christian Faith* was shaped by his setting out from what he called "the religious self-consciousness." Karl Barth's theology in *Church Dogmatics* was shaped by his opening declaration that "dogmatics is the scientific self-examination of the Christian Church with respect to the content of its distinctive talk about God,"[2] the content of that distinctive talk being, so Barth argued, the Word of God, that is, Jesus Christ.

Anyone who composes a treatise on Christian theology could write, as his or her final sentence, "This is the God we Christians worship." Aquinas could have written those words as the final sentence of *Summa Theologiae*, Calvin could have written them as the final sentence of *The Institutes of the Christian Religion*, Schleiermacher could have written them as the final sentence of *The Christian Faith*. Christian theology is about the God Christians worship. There is no other. There are not two gods, one whom Christian theologians write about and one whom Christians worship.

In setting as my topic, *The God We Worship*, I did not have in mind to develop a systematic theology of one or another of the above configurations at the end of which I could append the sentence, "This is the God we Christians worship." Rather than appending a reference to worship, I will begin with worship; and rather than making a passing reference to worship, I will aim at making explicit the understanding of God implicit in Christian worship and then, at a few points, to articulate that understanding, that is, to explain it, develop and elaborate it, and defend it. My project is liturgical theology.

As such, my project is both similar to, and significantly different from, Karl Barth's project in *Church Dogmatics*. Barth also starts from the Christian liturgy. But while recognizing that there is more to liturgy than proclamation, which he understands as speech about God, Barth focuses exclusively on proclamation. And while recognizing that proclamation does not only occur in preaching and the sacraments, Barth focuses on those. Of those two, preaching gets the lion's share of attention. Dogmatic

---

2. Karl Barth, *Church Dogmatics*, Volume 1, Part 1: *The Doctrine of the Word of God*, ed. T. F. Torrance, trans. G. W. Bromiley (Edinburgh: T&T Clark, 1975), p. 3.

theology, for Barth, was essentially critical reflection on the content of the church's preaching.

Whereas Barth focused on preaching, my attention will be on liturgy as a whole. And whereas Barth saw theology as that site where the church, by means of the work of its theologians, carries out a critical *Wissenschaft-lich* self-examination of the content of its proclamation, liturgical theology, as I understand it, is that site where the church, by means of the work of its theologians and philosophers, arrives at a self-understanding of the theology implicit and explicit in its liturgy. The liturgical theologian, on behalf of the church, is free to critically examine that theology when and where such examination seems called for. But liturgical theology aims, first of all, not at self-examination by the church of its liturgy but at self-understanding by the church of the theology implicit and explicit in its liturgy.

In this respect, liturgical theology is similar to what I called *conciliar* or *creedal* theology. I take Augustine's *De Trinitate* to be a paradigmatic example of this sort of theology. In that book, Augustine articulates those parts of the church's creeds and conciliar declarations that speak of the Trinity; he does not, in the first instance, critically examine the doctrine of the Trinity as formulated in those creeds and declarations. He explains the doctrine, develops and elaborates it, defends it. In the Afterword of this volume I will have more to say about the similarity of liturgical theology to conciliar or creedal theology.

What Is Christian Liturgy?

To explain, in more detail, how I understand the project of liturgical theology and why I think it worth undertaking, we must begin with some comments on the nature of the Christian liturgy. Of course, strictly speaking there is no such thing as *the* Christian liturgy; there are only Christian *liturgies,* in the plural. However, among the liturgies of the Orthodox Church, the Catholic Church, the Episcopal Church, the Lutheran churches, and the Reformed and Presbyterian churches, there is a good deal of convergence. I will concentrate on the points of convergence among these liturgies — not on their idiosyncrasies but on the similarities. At the end of this chapter I will explain why I have chosen to focus on the points of convergence among these particular liturgies rather than some others.

It is my judgment, shared by many, that the Russian Orthodox theologian, Alexander Schmemann, was the finest liturgical theologian of the

Orthodox Church in the twentieth century. In the opening chapter of his *Introduction to Liturgical Theology,*[3] Schmemann, speaking of the liturgical revival movement that took place in Orthodoxy, Catholicism, and various parts of Protestantism in the latter part of the nineteenth century and the first half or so of the twentieth, says that the "substance [of the movement] lies in the genuine discovery of worship as the life of the church, the public act which eternally actualizes the nature of the Church as the Body of Christ" (12). Speaking more specifically of the Orthodox Church in the next chapter, he says, "the worship of the Orthodox Church is conducted according to Ordo, that is, according to definite regulations" (28). In the comments about liturgy that follow in this chapter, my goal is to arrive at the place where we can understand what Schmemann is saying here and can see that it holds for Christian liturgies in general, not just for the Orthodox liturgy.

Let me begin with some comments on what might be called the *ontology* of liturgy. The ontology of liturgy proves more complex than one might initially surmise.

The term "liturgy" is often used to refer to a text; a liturgy, on this usage, is something one can hold in one's hand. This is a perfectly correct way of using the term. But when those who participated in the liturgical revival movement of the nineteenth and twentieth centuries used the term "liturgy," it was usually not one or another liturgical text that they were referring to. A liturgical text exists not for its own sake but for the sake of enactments of the liturgy. The text guides enactments, in the same way that the text for a drama guides performances of the drama and the score for a musical work guides performances of the work. When Schmemann speaks of liturgy as *actualizing* the church, it is enactments of the liturgy that he has in mind.

On the other hand, when he refers to the liturgy of the Orthodox Church it is something else that he has in mind, not any particular liturgical enactment. Which one would that be? He is referring to something that has been repeatedly enacted, with only minor variations, Sunday after Sunday for hundreds of years in multiple places.

Anything that can be repeatedly and multiply enacted is a universal. The Orthodox liturgy is a universal. More specifically, it's a type, a type whose enactments or instantiations consist of sequences of actions of cer-

---

3. Alexander Schmemann, *Introduction to Liturgical Theology* (Crestwood, NY: St. Vladimir's Seminary Press, 1966). Subsequent references to this book will be incorporated into the text.

tain kinds. And so too for the contemporary Catholic liturgy, the various contemporary Episcopal liturgies, the various contemporary Presbyterian liturgies, and all the others. One and all, they are capable of being repeatedly enacted. One and all, they are universals. One and all, they are types of sequences of actions of certain kinds.

The kinds of actions that go to make up one of these types of sequences always include bodily actions of various kinds; when the assembly enacts its liturgy, the members of the assembly do things with their bodies. Prominent among these bodily actions are listening, speaking, and singing. But the prominence of those should not lead us to overlook the fact that there are many others as well: standing, kneeling, processing, crossing oneself, distributing bread and wine, eating bread and drinking wine, sprinkling with water, dunking in water, closing one's eyes, dropping money in a container, washing, kissing, prostrating, and more besides.

On the other hand, it is by no means the case that all the actions performed in the enactment of a Christian liturgy are bodily actions. Mainly this is true because performances of many of the bodily actions count as performances of actions that are not bodily. The priest, at the beginning of an enactment in English of the Orthodox liturgy of John Chrysostom, pronounces the words, "Blessed be the kingdom of the Father, and of the Son, and of the Holy Spirit, now, and ever, and for evermore." The priest's pronouncing of those words is a bodily action; the priest uses his mouth and vocal chords to perform the action. But his performance of the bodily action of pronouncing those words *counts as* his doing something else, namely, blessing the kingdom of the holy Trinity. And that act of blessing is not a bodily action. I will be developing this point in Chapter Five.

The next point to be made about the ontology of liturgy can best be made, I think, by first making some observations about music and then pointing to the similarities of liturgy to music. When a composer writes a score for a musical composition, what he essentially does is institute a set of rules for a correct musical performance; now there is a new way for a musical performance to be correct. What the composer writes down in the score never specifies the complete set of rules, however; the composer always takes for granted certain rules for correctness that are embedded in the musical culture of the time — rules for correctness in playing the violin, for example. Let me call the total set of correctness-rules that the composer institutes, both those specified in the score and those he takes for granted, the *script* for the composition. I am, of course, stretching the ordinary meaning of the word "script."

The musical work itself that the composer has composed, in distinction from the set of rules that constitutes the script, is a type of sequence of sounds of certain kinds. Specifically, the musical work is the sound-sequence type that is instantiated when the correctness-rules that the composer has instituted are faithfully followed. It is the sequence-type of sounds of certain kinds that is instantiated in correct performances. Since the musical work can be instantiated in multiple performances, it's a universal.

An important part of the conceptuality that we use for thinking and talking about music is that a musical work can be performed not only correctly but also incorrectly. It is performed incorrectly when, at some point, the correctness-rules that the composer instituted are not faithfully followed. An incorrect performance of a work is still a performance of the work. On the other hand, it does sometimes happen that a performance departs so far from the relevant correctness-rules, the script, that we judge it not to be a performance of the work at all.

Corresponding to the script, and to the work of music that the script determines, there is a certain know-how on the part of musicians; specifically, the know-how of knowing how to perform the work correctly and, beyond that, of knowing how to perform it well. In our musical culture, knowing how to perform one work of music correctly and well comes along with knowing how to perform a wide range of works correctly and well.

Certain know-hows are such that it's possible to pick them up on one's own and never bother to transmit them to anyone else. There was something wrong with the start-up on my computer. All on my own I discovered a roundabout way of starting it up; there hasn't been any occasion to transmit my know-how to anybody else.

Music is very different. A young, would-be musician does not pick up on her own the know-how for performing a certain range of musical works correctly and well; she acquires that know-how by being inducted into the social practice for the exercise of this particular know-how. There are others who possess the know-how; musical know-how is a shared know-how. And the know-how is picked up by young, would-be, musicians from those who already possess the know-how. Musical know-how is handed on; there is a tradition of musical know-how — or to speak more precisely, there are traditions, in the plural.

With these points in mind, let us now look at liturgy. Consider the text for some liturgy, for example, the text for The Holy Eucharist: Rite

One, contained in the Episcopal *Book of Common Prayer.* That text specifies a set of rules for a correct liturgical enactment. But just as a musical score never specifies the full set of correctness-rules for a musical performance, so also the liturgical text for The Holy Eucharist: Rite One, does not specify the complete set of rules for its enactment; some are to be found in the liturgical culture of the Episcopal Church. As in the case of music, let's call the complete set of rules for a correct liturgical enactment, both those specified in the liturgical text and those to be found in the relevant liturgical culture, the *script* for the liturgy.

When discussing music I might have mentioned that, for some musical works, there is no score and never has been; the entire set of correctness-rules is to be found in the relevant part of the musical culture. So too with liturgy; for some liturgies, there is no text and never has been. None of the correctness-rules has ever been written down; the entire set is to be found in the relevant liturgical culture. No part of the script has ever been inscribed. The liturgies that I will be discussing are not of that sort; for each of them, a good deal of the script has been inscribed.

The eucharistic liturgy that the Episcopal Church designates as "The Holy Eucharist: Rite One," in distinction from the script for that liturgy, is the sequence-type of actions of certain kinds that is instantiated when the script for that liturgy is faithfully followed, so that a correct enactment comes about. As with music, an important part of the conceptuality that we use for thinking and talking about liturgy is that a liturgy can be enacted not only correctly but also incorrectly.

To participate in the enactment of a liturgy is thus to perform scripted, rule-governed, actions, just as to participate in the performance of some work of music is to perform scripted, rule-governed, actions. That's what Schmemann was alluding to when he said that "the worship of the Orthodox Church is conducted according to . . . definite regulations." What Schmemann calls the "regulations" for the Orthodox liturgy I am calling the *script.* And the Orthodox liturgy itself just is the liturgy for which those correctness-rules are the script; the Orthodox liturgy is the liturgy that is enacted when that script is faithfully followed.

Corresponding to the script for a liturgy, and corresponding to the liturgy itself which that particular set of correctness-rules determines, there is a certain know-how on the part of those who participate in enactments of that liturgy; specifically, the know-how of knowing how to enact the liturgy correctly and, beyond that, of knowing how to enact it well. This liturgical know-how differs from the corresponding musical know-how in that it is a less generalized know-how. The know-how of a trained pianist puts him in the position of knowing how to perform both Beethoven's Piano Sonata Opus 106 and Schubert's Sonata D 960 — though if he has never played these, he may have to acquire a few digital skills in order to implement his know-how. Not so for liturgy. Liturgical know-how approaches being tradition-specific. If one has the know-how for participating in an enactment of Rite One of the Episcopal Church, then one also has the know-how for participating in an enactment of Rite Two. But the know-how that enables one to participate in the enactment of one or another of the Episcopal liturgies is not a know-how that enables one to participate in an enactment of the Orthodox Liturgy of John Chrysostom. Naturally one is not completely lacking in know-how. But if one has never before attended an enactment of the Orthodox liturgy, best to look around and observe how it's done.

Be that as it may, liturgy is like music in that one acquires some particular liturgical know-how by being inducted into a social practice for the exercise of this know-how. There are others who possess the know-how in question; liturgical know-how is a shared know-how. And the know-how is acquired by those who do not have it from those who do. Liturgical know-how is handed on; there's a tradition of a particular liturgical know-how.

In principle one can worship God without following any script and without having acquired any relevant know-how by induction into some social practice. I think this happens less often than one might initially suppose, however; almost all of us, in worshipping God, follow a script and have acquired at least some of our know-how from others. Nonetheless, it seems possible that someone would read a few passages from the New Testament and begin worshipping the God of whom she has read without following any rules for correctness and being completely ignorant of those ways of worshipping God that Christians have passed on to each other.

If this is correct, then Christian liturgical actions are best thought of as one species of acts of Christian worship — an exceedingly prominent species, indeed, but only a species. Acts of worship are liturgical when they are scripted. Most liturgical worship is communal; in talking about liturgy, Schmemann has his eye exclusively on communal worship. But liturgical worship, as I have just now explained it, need not be communal. One can follow a script in one's private devotions; many people do. I suggest that Christian worship is liturgical when it is — to repeat — the scripted performance of acts of worship.

On one of my trips to China I became acquainted with some young Chinese Christians for whom, so far as I could tell, worship was not part of their Christian life. So far as I could tell, Christianity for them was a religious orientation that included love for neighbor, this in turn generating critique of the government; but it did not include worship.

There are individual Christians like that scattered around the globe, people who identify themselves as Christian but seldom if ever engage in worship. However, I know of no body of Christians who get together for worship whose worship does not take the form of liturgical worship. In some non-denominational free-church congregations there may be no trace of a liturgical text, nothing written down. Nonetheless, there is a script for doing it right. Even in such congregations there can be mistakes; even in such congregations worship takes the form of scripted action, if for no other reason than to forestall chaos and a babel of voices. And always the people will share a certain know-how that they have acquired from others and that they, in turn, can and often do hand on to others.

Liturgy as Actualization of the Church

I introduced my discussion of liturgy by saying that I would aim at arriving at a place where we could discern not only the meaning but the plausibility, for liturgy in general, of two comments made by Alexander Schmemann: one, that the church actualizes herself in the enactment of the liturgy, the other, that the Orthodox liturgy is conducted according to an Ordo, that is, according to definite regulations. What Schmemann calls the "Ordo" of the Orthodox liturgy I call "the script." And I have argued that all liturgies, not just the Orthodox, have a script; to participate in the enactment of some liturgy is to engage in scripted action.

What remains obscure is what Schmemann means when he says that the church *actualizes* herself in her enactment of the liturgy. Earlier I suggested that it has something to do with understanding liturgy as consisting not of liturgical texts but as a way of doing something. But that falls short of fully explaining what Schmemann means.

Just as I judge Schmemann to be the finest twentieth-century liturgical theologian of the Orthodox Church, so I judge the Swiss theologian J.-J. von Allmen to be the finest twentieth-century liturgical theologian of the Reformed tradition. In the opening chapters of his magnum opus, *Worship: Its Theology and Practice,* von Allmen offers three distinct "takes"

9

on the Christian liturgy.[4] The Christian liturgy, he says, is the recapitulation of the history of salvation, it is the epiphany of the church, and it is the end and future of the world. I interpret what von Allmen has in mind when he describes the liturgy as the epiphany of the church as essentially the same as what Schmemann had in mind when he described the liturgy as the actualization of the church. About liturgy as the epiphany of the church von Allmen says this: "by its worship the Church becomes itself, becomes conscious of itself, and confesses itself as a distinct entity" (42).

To describe the enactment of the liturgy as the *epiphany* of the church is about as obscure, however, as to describe it as the *actualization* of the church. What might Schmemann and von Allmen have in mind? What they have in mind begins to become clear when Schmemann sets his view over against an opposing view that he finds common among his Orthodox brothers and sisters:

> The fact is that worship has ceased to be understood as a function of the Church. . . . In the contemporary approach to worship there is the characteristic absence of an understanding of it as the expression of the Church, as the creation of the Church and as the fulfilment of the Church. The Church has been merged with worship, has come to be understood as a sacramentally hierarchical institution existing for the performance of divine worship seen as a sacred, supra-temporal, immutable mystery. . . . The Church cannot express, create and fulfil herself in [worship] because outside the mystery there is no Church. There are separate believers, to a greater or lesser extent living individually by sacred contact with it, by the sanctification or nourishment received from it. . . . [T]he individual believer, entering the church, does not feel he is a participant and celebrant of worship, does not know that in this act of worship he, along with the others who together with him are constituting the Church, is called to express the Church as new life and to be transformed again into a member of the Church. He has become an "object" of worship, it is celebrated for his "nourishment," so that he may as an individual satisfy his "religious needs." . . . [T]he purpose of the cult is thought of precisely as the bestowal of a spiritual experience, spiritual food. For

---

4. J.-J. von Allmen, *Worship: Its Theology and Practice* (London: Lutterworth Press, 1965). The translation from the original French is by Harold Knight and W. Fletcher Fleet. Hereafter, references to this work will be incorporated into the text.

the membership of the Church worship has ceased to be the Church's self-evidencing. (23-25)

I take Schmemann's point to be the following. Many members of the church think of it as a service organization catering to their religious or spiritual needs and desires. The clergy enact the liturgy for the benefit of those who find it spiritually nourishing and edifying. It is to this functional understanding of the church that Schmemann is deeply opposed — as is von Allmen.

Both insist that the liturgy is not something enacted by the clergy for the purpose of satisfying the needs and desires of the congregants, be those needs and desires spiritual, emotional, aesthetic, or whatever. It's the church that enacts the liturgy, not the clergy. Though the church does so under the leadership of the clergy, the liturgy is not something that clerics do. And the church enacts the liturgy not to satisfy the needs and desires of individual congregants but to worship God. The church blesses God, praises God, thanks God, confesses her sins to God, petitions God, listens to God's Word, celebrates the Eucharist. It's not the individual members who do these things simultaneously; it's the assembled body that does these things.

Further, these are not just to be numbered among the many good things that the church does; it was for the performance of such actions that God created the church. When the church assembles for communal worship, she does what she was called into existence to do. The church exists to worship God in Christ. It is in this sense that, in enacting the liturgy, she actualizes herself; and in actualizing herself, she manifests herself. The liturgy, to use von Allmen's term, is an epiphany of the church.

It's important to add that neither Schmemann nor von Allmen was of the view that the church exists only for the purpose of worship and that it is only in worship that she actualizes herself. The church is called to acknowledge God throughout her existence, not only when gathered for worship but also in her life in the everyday. Schmemann does tend to talk as if outside the liturgy it is individual Christians who act, not the church. But in his little book, *For the Life of the World*,[5] he powerfully develops the point that the life of the Christian is to be conducted in such a way as to be, as a whole, an acknowledgment of who God is and of what God has done.

Both Schmemann and von Allmen are of the view, however, that it is especially in the enactment of the liturgy, rather than in the work of the

---

5. Alexander Schmemann, *For the Life of the World* (Crestwood, NY: St. Vladimir's Seminary Press, 1998).

faithful in the world, that the nature and purpose of the church become manifest. I think they are right about that.

Though I affirm what I have interpreted Schmemann as meaning when he says that in the enactment of the liturgy the church actualizes herself, and what I have interpreted von Allmen as meaning when he says that the enactment of the liturgy is the epiphany of the church, I think it is important not to stop there but to go on immediately to add another note. In the enactment of the liturgy not only does the church act in such a way as to actualize and manifest herself; God also acts. Both Schmemann and von Allmen affirm this point in their writing. But I think we run the risk of serious distortion if we do not, in the same breath that we say that the church actualizes and manifests herself in the liturgy, also say that God acts in the liturgy. This will prove important for my discussion in subsequent chapters.

On Making the Implicit Explicit

Let me now move on to explain what I have in mind when I describe my project as making explicit the understanding of God implicit in the Christian liturgy. Suppose that an early Christian liturgy had come about by a Christian of theological sophistication composing a liturgy that gave expression to his theological convictions. For example, having concluded from the Resurrection, Pentecost, and various things Jesus said, that God was in some inexplicable way intimately related to Jesus and the Spirit, a conclusion shared with other early Christians, he might have included, as the opening or closing of his liturgy, something like the final verse of Paul's Second Letter to the Corinthians: "The grace of the Lord Jesus Christ, the love of God, and the fellowship of the Holy Spirit, be with you all." And, believing that we wrong God by our disobedience and indifference, he might have included a prayer for forgiveness on the model of that to be found in the paradigmatic prayer that Jesus gave to his disciples.

If we had been around at the time, we could have asked him to spell out for us the theological convictions that shaped his liturgy. Some of those convictions would have received explicit expression in the liturgy and would already have been apparent to us, for example, the proto-trinitarianism of that Pauline greeting. But others would have remained implicit, for example, the conviction that God can be wronged. It's highly unlikely that our theologian would have explicitly stated in the liturgy that God can be wronged; he would simply have composed a prayer for forgiveness. So in responding to our request to spell out for us the theological convictions that shaped his liturgy, he would have mentioned his conviction that we wrong God, and would have noted that it was for this reason that he included a prayer for forgiveness in his liturgical composition. Of course, he would almost certainly not have been fully conscious of all the ways in which his theology shaped his liturgy.

What I have described is pure fantasy. All the evidence points to the fact that the early Christian liturgies were not composed but emerged and developed organically, mainly from two sources: the readings and prayers of the Jewish synagogue, and what transpired in the Upper Room when Jesus ate his last supper. Until the invention of printing, when liturgical texts became common, liturgy continued to change and develop organically under a multiplicity of influences. Under the influence of theological convictions, to be sure; but also under the influence of practices of the Roman imperial court, practices of the Byzantine imperial court, changing views concerning the status of the clergy, the need to exclude the non-catechized and non-baptized from the Eucharist, and so forth, on and on.

Eventually some leaders of the church did do what one might call "compose a liturgy." Possibly St. Basil composed the liturgy that the Orthodox know as The Liturgy of St. Basil, and possibly John Chrysostom composed the liturgy that they know as The Liturgy of St. John Chrysostom, though in neither case is the evidence on the matter decisive. We do know that Calvin composed a liturgy for his church in Strasbourg. But the best-known example of liturgical composition is Thomas Cranmer's composition of the liturgy in the original *Book of Common Prayer.*

Neither Calvin nor Cranmer began from scratch in composing their liturgy, in the way that Beethoven began from scratch in composing, say, his Fifth Symphony. Neither has anyone else who has composed a liturgy begun from scratch. No one who has composed a liturgy has ever done anything more than compose a revision of liturgies that were themselves not composed but developed organically under a multiplicity of influences from many different quarters.

Had we been around at the time, we could have asked Cranmer, himself a sophisticated theologian, to spell out for us the theological convictions that led him to revise earlier liturgies as he did into the liturgy of the *Book of Common Prayer.* His answer would have gone some way toward articulating the understanding of God explicit and implicit in his liturgy. But since his liturgy was not a start-from-scratch composition, since much of it was just taken over, almost certainly he would not have been fully aware of all the theology implicit in his liturgy.

Since no liturgy has ever been composed from scratch, there's no one we can ask, concerning any of the traditional liturgies, to spell out for us the theological convictions that went into composing the liturgy as they did. We can get partial answers from Cranmer and his like, as we can nowadays from the members of liturgical revision committees; but the answers we get are never anything more than partial. Liturgical revision committees will generally be quite conscious of the theological convictions shaping the revisions they make; they will be less conscious, or not at all conscious, of the theological convictions implicit in what they take over from their predecessors.

But how then do we identify the theological understandings implicit in the liturgy? No problem identifying those that are explicit. The present-day Episcopal liturgy opens with the celebrant saying, "Blessed be God: Father, Son, and Holy Spirit."[6] God is explicitly understood here as Trinity, that's obvious. But God is also implicitly understood as being of a sort whom it is appropriate to bless. The celebrant doesn't declare that God is a being of that sort; and so, of course, the celebrant doesn't specify what it is about God that makes it appropriate to bless God. He or she just goes ahead and blesses God.

In the Anaphora of the Orthodox liturgy, which comes just before the eucharistic meal, the priest, addressing God, declares God to be "ineffable, beyond comprehension, invisible, beyond understanding, ever-existing and always the same."[7] Here God is explicitly identified as ineffable, inconceivable, and so forth. What remains implicit is that God is understood as one whom it is appropriate to address. Nowhere in the liturgy is this stated, and hence nowhere is there an explanation as to what it is about God that makes it appropriate for the people to address God. They just go ahead and address God.

A question that comes to mind here is whether, instead of asking what is the understanding of God implicit in the liturgy, we could just as well ask what the participants in the liturgy take for granted about God when participating in an enactment of the liturgy. The answer is, No. What people take for granted in participating in the liturgy varies from person to person. To take the extreme case: some people don't take anything at all about God for granted in participating in the liturgy because they don't

---

6. *Book of Common Prayer,* p. 323.

7. An Orthodox friend of mine described this to me as "apophaticism in high gear." The English translation that I will be using is by Rev. Nicon D. Patrinacos (Garwood, NJ: Graphic Arts Press, 1974). Subsequent references to this edition of the Orthodox liturgy will be incorporated into the text. The acclamation quoted above is on p. 45.

believe in God. They realize, of course, that there is a lot of God-talk in the liturgy. But they don't take such talk seriously. They participate because they find that doing so serves the cause of self-improvement in some way: they find themselves morally strengthened, psychologically calmed, centered, drawn to beauty. Their participation is what I shall call *deviant;* they do not participate in order to perform the actions of the liturgy. So too, the participation in the liturgy of ancient Israel that the prophets excoriated was a *deviant* participation.

A script for the Christian liturgy is a script for those to follow who have assembled to worship the Christian God. The script specifies a sequence of actions to be performed. Those actions are not just the utterance of certain words or the making of certain gestures. They are the uttering of certain words and *saying something thereby,* or the making of certain gestures and *doing something else thereby.* The opening words for the Episcopal liturgy are, once again, these, pronounced by the celebrant: "Blessed be God: Father, Son, and Holy Spirit." What the script specifies for the opening of an enactment of this liturgy is not just that the celebrant utter those words but that the celebrant *bless* God *by* uttering those words. It's a nice question, discussed at length in earlier times, whether a celebrant who does not believe in God, or who does not believe in blessing God, has nonetheless blessed God by uttering those words. For our purposes it's not necessary to get into that issue. Sufficient to note that such participation would be deviant and that, whatever the celebrant may or may not have done, what the script for the liturgy specifies is that the celebrant bless God by uttering the words, "Blessed be God: Father, Son, and Holy Spirit." My interest in what follows is not in making explicit what is implicit in whatever it is that the celebrant has done, or in what he or she takes for granted, but in making explicit what is implicit in the action specified by the script for the opening of the liturgy.

Once again then: what are we trying to do when we try to make explicit — to identify and formulate — the understanding of God implicit in the liturgy? What is it to make the implicit explicit?

The task of liturgical theology, says Schmemann in his *Introduction to Liturgical Theology,* is to uncover the theological "logos" of the liturgy (32), its theological "meaning" (18, and *passim*). The liturgy, he says, contains theology "in code"; the task of the liturgical theologian is to "decode" the code (18), "to translate what is expressed by the language of worship — its structures, its ceremonies, its texts and its whole 'spirit' — into the language of theology" (19). In liturgical theology, the liturgical tradition arrives at "dogmatic consciousness" (16). What Schmemann describes here as "decoding" the theology that the liturgy contains is the same as what I call *making explicit* the understanding of God implicit in the liturgy.

Given a particular liturgy, always some of what it "says" about God will be explicit. But always much of it will be implicit. To make the implicit explicit, we start from some particular liturgical act, or from some type of liturgical act, or from the liturgy as a whole, and we ask what God would have to be like for it to make sense to perform this particular liturgical act, or to perform liturgical acts of this type, or to perform the liturgy as a whole. What would God have to be like for it to make sense for us to bless God? What would God have to be like for it to make sense for us to address God, whatever the content of our address? What would God have to be like for it to make sense to worship God in the way that Christians do? It is by asking such questions that we make explicit — identify and formulate — the understanding of God implicit in the liturgy. It is by asking such questions that we make explicit what Schmemann calls the theological "logos" of the liturgy.

An interesting example of liturgical theology from the Church Fathers is Basil of Caesarea's little book, *On the Holy Spirit*. Here is what Basil says in introducing his discussion:

> Lately while I pray with the people, we sometimes finish the doxology to God the Father with the form "Glory to the Father *with* the Son, *together with* the Holy Spirit," and at other times we use "Glory to the Father *through the* Son *in* the Holy Spirit." Some of those present accused us of using strange and mutually contradictory terms. But your wish certainly is to help these people, or, if they should prove completely incurable, to safeguard those who associate with them; that is why you [Amphilochius] think that clear teaching concerning the force underlying these prepositions is desirable. I will write as concisely as possible, hoping to present a suitable beginning for this discussion.[8]

Basil then proceeds to defend his practice of praying in both ways and to make explicit and articulate the understanding of the Holy Spirit implicit in the words he uses.

---

8. St. Basil the Great, *On the Holy Spirit,* trans. David Anderson (Crestwood, NY: St. Vladimir's Seminary Press, 1980). I thank Kevin Hector for calling this book by Basil to my attention.

The Project More Precisely Characterized

There's more to the implicit logos of the liturgy than an implicit understanding of God; there's also an implicit understanding of the participants, of human beings in general, and of the world. For example, implicit in asking God for forgiveness is that we are of such a sort as to make it appropriate for us to ask God for forgiveness. Also implicit in the liturgy, as Schmemann points out at some length, is a certain understanding of time. It would be worth exploring these and other aspects of the implied logos of the liturgy. However, in the chapters that follow I will focus exclusively on the implied theological logos of the liturgy — that is, on the understanding of *God* implicit in the liturgy.

It would also be worthwhile to ask what the liturgy as a whole says about God, not just what it says implicitly but also what it says explicitly. I will focus on what the liturgy says *implicitly* about God. I have two reasons for this. First, what a liturgy says explicitly about God is relatively obvious as compared to what it says implicitly. We can go on to develop and elaborate the explicit understanding, defend it against objections, and so forth; but identifying and formulating it is relatively easy. Second, the explicit presupposes the implicit. Blessing God with explicitly trinitarian language presupposes that God is the sort of being whom it is appropriate to bless. My project is to uncover the fundamental presuppositions of the Christian liturgy.

The understanding of God implicit in the liturgy can be thought of as coming in four levels. The deepest level is the understanding of God 12. implicit in the liturgy as a whole. The understanding of God implicit in the Christian liturgy as a whole is significantly different, for example, from the understanding of God implicit in the temple liturgy of ancient Israel.

2. The next level up is the understanding of God implicit in the various types of liturgical acts. For example, in both the liturgical act of praising God and the liturgical act of interceding with God, the people address God. Thus, deeper than the understanding of God implicit in praising God and deeper than that implicit in interceding with God is the understanding of God implicit in that type of act of which these are both species, namely, an act of addressing God.

3. The next level up is the understanding of God implicit in particular liturgical actions — in our praise of God, in our blessing of God, in our intercessions, and so forth.

4. The final level is the understanding of God implicit in the sequence of liturgical actions, that is, the way they are ordered sequentially. In tra-

ditional Reformed and Presbyterian liturgies, the confession of sins occurs very early, right after the opening greeting and hymn of praise and before the reading of Scripture; in the Episcopal liturgy it occurs much later, after the reading of Scripture, the sermon, and the prayers of the people, just before the Eucharist proper.[9] Presumably there is a somewhat different understanding of God implicit in these strikingly different sequences, or perhaps a different understanding of our relation to God.

In what follows I will be focusing almost entirely on the two deepest levels of implicitness: what is implicit in the Christian liturgy as a whole, and what is implicit in the basic types of liturgical acts. Only when we get to the understanding of God implicit in the Eucharist will our focus be on the third level. And I will not have anything to say about what is implicit in the way liturgical actions are ordered sequentially.

My description of what it is to make explicit the understanding of God implicit in the liturgy may have given the impression that it's easy to understand what goes on in one and another liturgical act, and that the hard work begins when we go beyond understanding the act itself to try to identify the understanding of God implicit in the act, and that the hard work continues when we then try to develop theologically the implicit understanding that we have made explicit and to defend it against objections.

The impression is mistaken. What we will discover is that often a lot of hard work goes into determining what is going on in the liturgical act itself; sometimes, when we have succeeded in doing that, the next step, that of identifying and formulating the understanding of God implicit in the act, proves relatively easy.

A consequence of the fact that sometimes it's not at all obvious what is going on in a certain liturgical act, that sometimes it requires a lot of hard work to arrive at an understanding of the act, is that the interpretation one arrives at often proves controversial. And sometimes those controversies turn out to have, as their root, theological disagreements. Theology does not enter the picture only after we have discerned what is taking place in some liturgical act and have moved on to try to make explicit, and to articulate theologically, the understanding of God implicit in that act. Different theological convictions often lead to different interpretations of what is going on in our liturgical actions.

---

9. There is, however, an implicit confession very near the opening of the Episcopal liturgy when the people say "Lord, have mercy upon us," in response to the celebrant's reading of the two love commands.

Why Deal Only with the Traditional Liturgies?

A question that's been waiting in the wings ever since the opening pages of this chapter is, why is liturgical theology worth doing? Why not content ourselves with the other types of theology described in the opening pages? I think it best to postpone answering this question until we have some actual liturgical theology in hand. In the Afterword to this book I will compare liturgical theology in some detail to other forms of theology and will point to the distinct contribution that it makes.

A question that does need to be addressed here, however, is why I have chosen to focus my attention on the points of convergence of the Orthodox liturgy, the Catholic liturgy, the Episcopal liturgy, the Lutheran liturgies, and the Reformed liturgies. Most Christians today enact one or another of these liturgies in their worship; but around the world, millions do not. Why not bring their liturgies into the picture as well?

I have three reasons for focusing on the traditional liturgies. One reason, about which I will have something more to say in the Afterword, is that the traditional liturgies have stood the test of time across many centuries by billions of Christians. For that reason, the understanding of God implicit and explicit in those liturgies has more authority, carries more weight *(gravitas),* than one composed on his own by, say, some Pentecostal pastor in Houston for next Sunday's service in his church; the theology implicit and explicit in the latter is more likely to be quirky, distorted, out of the mainstream.[10]

Second, the script of many of these alternative liturgies changes from week to week, usually in accord with the preferences of the pastor; and when it does not change from week to week, usually much less of the script is written down than is the case for traditional liturgies. What this implies is that it is much more difficult for the scholar to gain access to these liturgies than to the traditional liturgies.

---

10. Here is what the Dutch Reformed theologian Abraham Kuyper (1837-1920) said about the importance of liturgical tradition: "A liturgical prayer is therefore not composed in just a few moments. In fact, it should come to us from the past and from the bosom of the church. The forms and expressions that through the centuries have given voice to the deepest and holiest promptings of the heart must be passed on from generation to generation and speak to the soul. Tone, language, and content should rise above any spontaneous prayer, and immerse us in the deep stream of the communion of saints." See Abraham Kuyper, *Our Worship,* ed. Harry Boonstra (Grand Rapids: William B. Eerdmans Publishing Company, 2009), p. 36.

Third, the traditional liturgies have a depth, a richness, a beauty that, in my experience, these contemporary alternative liturgies lack. In my (admittedly limited) experience, the latter liturgies strip elements out of the traditional liturgies, reduce the imagery, make the language chatty and prosaic so that everyone can understand immediately what is being said. There remains only a faint echo of the enormous devotion and creativity that the early church poured into its liturgies. The most radical example of this reductive flattening-out that I have encountered was a Sunday morning service that consisted of nothing more than a praise band performing for about half an hour, followed by a perfunctory prayer spoken by the leader of the band and what was described as a "talk" by the minister — nothing more.

If the alternative contemporary liturgies that I have experienced are typical of these liturgies as a whole, then these liturgies do not represent a fresh burst of liturgical creativity but represent instead the stripping out from the traditional liturgies of almost all their components. Accordingly, in discussing the theological implications of the acts to be found in the traditional liturgies we are also discussing the acts to be found in these alternative contemporary liturgies, since there are none to be found in the latter that are not to be found in the former.

My focus on the traditional liturgies does, of course, pose a question to the alternative contemporary liturgies, namely, why have they stripped so many things out?[11] Why was there no confession of sins in that service I mentioned? Why no intercessions? Why no reading of Scripture? And why was there almost no sense of the majesty and awesomeness of God? Is there an understanding of God implicit in this radical stripping out that is different from the understanding to be found in the traditional liturgies? If so, what is that different understanding? Obviously these questions are important; however, in this text I will not be able to address them. It will be the richer traditional liturgies that I will be considering.

11. I should add here that the revisions of their traditional liturgies that all denominations, with the exception of the Orthodox, undertook in the twentieth century also amounted to the stripping out of a fair number of traditional elements and theological principles.

CHAPTER TWO

God as Worthy of Worship

My project in this book is to make explicit the understanding of God implicit in the Christian liturgy and then to make a beginning at developing and elaborating those understandings theologically.

In explaining the project, I distinguished four levels of implicitness: the understanding of God implicit in the liturgy as a whole, the understanding of God implicit in the basic types of our various liturgical actions, the understanding of God implicit in specific liturgical actions, and the understanding of God implicit in how our liturgical actions are sequentially ordered. I begin, in this chapter, at the deepest level of implicitness, namely, with the understanding of God implicit in the Christian liturgy as a whole — implicit in all our liturgical actions, whatever their type, whatever their specific character, and whatever their sequence. What is the understanding of God implicit in the liturgy as a whole? What does our enactment of the liturgy implicitly "say" about God?

Down through the centuries human beings have assembled to enact religious rituals for many different reasons, each of those reasons implying a somewhat different understanding of God or the gods. Sometimes it's thought that the gods are angry and that the rituals will propitiate or appease them. Sometimes the thought is not that the gods are presently angry but that they might become angry. The rituals serve to forestall the gods becoming angry; they serve to keep the gods well-disposed toward us. Either way, it's assumed that God or the gods will find the rituals pleasing.

Reading between the lines of some of the prophetic denunciations in the Old Testament, the idea that the rituals are for pleasing God seems to have been common in ancient Israel. Recall the well-known passage in Amos. God is the speaker:

I hate, I despise your festivals,
   and I take no delight in your solemn assemblies.
Even though you offer me your burnt offerings and grain offerings,
   I will not accept them;
and the offerings of well-being of your fatted animals
   I will not look upon.
Take away from me the noise of your songs;
   I will not listen to the melody of your harps.
But let justice roll down like waters,
   and the doing of what is right like an everflowing stream.

                     (Amos 5:21-24)[1]

If the Reformers of the sixteenth century were right in their denunciations of the lay Catholic piety of the day, a version of the idea that
ritual or liturgy is for pleasing God was widespread at the time. Participation in the liturgy was thought of as compensatory. In our daily lives
we all do what is wrong; we sin. God takes note, and in the ledger that
God sets up for each of us, God inscribes our sins on the negative side
of the ledger. But God also takes note of our good deeds; in particular,
God takes note of our participation in the liturgy, especially our participation in the Eucharist. God inscribes those acts on the positive side of
our ledger. One's overall goal is to see to it that, when one dies, what is
inscribed on the positive side of one's ledger outweighs what is inscribed
on the negative side.

Engaging in ritual activity in order to please the gods, thereby pla-
cating them, forestalling their ill-will, or compensating for the wrong one
has done, is only one among the many rationales that human beings have
embraced for enacting their rituals or liturgies. I have singled out this particular rationale so as to have before us a contrast with the fundamental
rationale for engaging in the Christian liturgy. For the purpose of contrast
I could, of course, have singled out any number of other rationales; for
example, nowadays one sometimes hears it said by someone who participates in the liturgy that she does so in order to "center" herself. What is
common to this and the rationale of pleasing God is that both focus on the
benefits that supposedly accrue to the participant.

In my opening chapter I took for granted that Christian liturgy is

---

1. Throughout this book, I am using both the NRSV and the RSV translations of the
Bible.

a species of Christian worship and devoted considerable time and effort to identifying the species; I concluded that to participate in the liturgy is to participate in the scripted enactment of some social practice for performing acts of Christian worship. It's possible, I said, to perform acts of Christian worship that are not scripted and that are not the enactment of some social practice for performing acts of Christian worship. That's why Christian liturgy is only a species of Christian worship.

Let me now affirm what previously I took for granted. When we assemble to participate in an enactment of the liturgy, we do so in order to worship God — not to please God, not to center ourselves, but to worship God. We may also do so because we expect or hope that we ourselves will be altered in some way, guided and energized for our life in the everyday, for example. But that's compatible with assembling in order to worship God; indeed if the alteration in ourselves that we expect or hope for comes about, it does so as a consequence of our engaging in worshipping God.

Worshipping God is not one among other things that we do when enacting the liturgy; worshipping God is the totality of what we do, apart, of course, from those ancillary actions in which the presider addresses the people, the people address the presider, and the congregants address each other. It follows that the understanding of God implicit in the liturgy as a whole is that God is worthy of worship. The deepest presupposition of the Christian liturgy is that God is worship-worthy.

Liturgy and Worship

What is worship? My *Merriam-Webster's Collegiate Dictionary* (11th edition) tells me that our word "worship" comes from the Middle English *worshipe,* meaning worthiness, respect, reverence paid to a divine being. And it says that the Middle English *worshipe* came from the Old English *weorthscipe,* meaning worthiness, respect. The term *weorthscipe* was a combination of the term *weorth,* meaning worth or worthy, with the suffix *-scipe.* To my ear, the term "worship" in present-day English remains true to its etymological origins: to worship God is to pay reverence to God for God's worth, to honor God for God's worth. But there is more that requires to be said than just that.

In general, worshipping someone is a mode of acknowledging that person's worthiness, that person's greatness or excellence. Thus worshipping God is a mode of acknowledging God's worthiness, the excellence of who God is and the greatness of what God has done, is doing, and will do. More specifically, in Christian worship we acknowledge the *unsurpassable* excellence of God.[2]

But acknowledging God's unsurpassable excellence is only the genus of Christian worship, not yet the species, for the reason that worshipping God is not the only way in which we acknowledge God's unsurpassable excellence. We can acknowledge God's unsurpassable greatness by our lives in the everyday — for example, by carrying out the prophetic call to imitate God by doing justice and loving mercy. But this is not worshipping God. Why not? What is it that is distinctive of worship?

What's distinctive, I would say, is the *orientation* that characterizes worship. In our lives in the everyday we are oriented toward our tasks, toward our neighbors, toward the created world. In assembling to worship God in the liturgy we turn around and orient ourselves toward God; we face God. In attending to the heavenly bodies we discern a manifestation of God's wisdom and power; in attending to the neighbor we discern the image of God. But in neither of such attendings do we *face* God. In worshipping God we turn away from attending to the heavenly bodies and away from attending to the neighbor so as to attend directly to God. In worship we are face to face with God. When we worship God, our acknowledgment of God's unsurpassable greatness is *Godward* in its orientation. We position our bodies accordingly: we kneel, we bow, we stand with face and hands upraised. There is no creature before whom we are kneeling or bowing; we are kneeling or bowing before God.

We are close to having identified that species of acknowledging God's excellence that is worship of God, but we're not quite there yet. In the course of a theological discourse about God, one might acknowledge God's unsurpassable excellence by describing that excellence; and in composing such a discourse one is, of course, oriented toward God. But composing a theological discourse on God's unsurpassable excellence would not, as such, be a case of worshipping God. Acknowledging God's unsurpassable excellence while oriented Godward may or may not be a case of worshipping God.

What's missing? What's missing is a certain *attitudinal stance* of the person toward God. In the absence of that distinct attitudinal stance, God-

---

2. I shall use the terms "worthiness," "excellence," and "greatness" interchangeably. As we shall see later in this chapter, Jonathan Edwards distinguished between God's greatness and God's excellence.

ward acknowledgment of God's unsurpassable excellence is not yet worship of God. It's the presence of a distinct attitudinal stance that makes one's Godward acknowledgment of God's unsurpassable excellence a case of worship.

By the term "attitudinal stance" I do not mean a feeling or emotion of some sort. The stance may include a feeling or emotion; but it's not to be identified with either of those. An attitudinal stance toward someone is a way of regarding that person. Regarding someone with admiration is an example of an attitudinal stance toward that person; regarding someone with disdain is another example.

The English term "adoration" seems to me to best capture the attitudinal stance of the worshipper toward God; our worship of God is our adoration of God. Adoration of something is a mode of love, specifically, love as attraction. To adore something is to be drawn to it on account of its worth, to be gripped by it; we speak of adoring some person, some work of art, some scene in nature. The actions that go to make up the Christian liturgy are actions expressive of adoration. I judge that the Orthodox liturgy, more than any other, gives explicit expression to the attitudinal stance of adoration. In the famous "Trisagion Hymn" the people say,

> Holy God,
> Holy and mighty,
> Holy and immortal one,
> have mercy on us. (p. 23)

After singing those lines three times, the people continue:

> Glory to the Father, and to the Son,
> and to the Holy Spirit;
> now, and ever, and for evermore. Amen.
> . . . Holy immortal one, have mercy on us.
> Holy God,
> Holy and mighty,
> Holy and immortal one,
> have mercy on us. (p. 25)

Adoration has somewhat different content depending on the object of adoration and on how the adoring person understands that object; adoration of a painting by Vincent van Gogh is different in its content from, say, adoration of some mathematical proof. So let us dig inside the Christian's worship and adoration of God so as to identify some of its content.

Our adoration of God for God's unsurpassable greatness incorporates being in *awe* of God's greatness. In the Orthodox liturgy, after the bread and wine have been brought into the sanctuary and the Eucharist proper is about to begin, the priest says, "Let us stand reverently, let us stand in awe" (43).

The content of our adoration of God includes more, however, than awe. One can be in awe of something without worshipping it. Recall the Bush administration's claim, when the invasion of Iraq was about to begin, that the bombing of Baghdad would produce shock and awe. Though the bombing did no doubt produce awe in some people, I feel confident in saying that in no one did it evoke adoration or worship. What has to be added? In our adoration of God, what more is there than awe? *Reverence,* I would say. "In reverence, let us stand before the Lord." Reverence is not the same as awe; nobody revered the bombing of Baghdad.

Without now making any claim to exhaustiveness, I suggest that the adoration definitive of Christian worship has yet a third component, namely, gratitude.[3] One would have to be dull indeed not to notice the prominence of gratitude in Christian worship.

Let me pull things together. I suggest that worship of God is a particular mode of Godward acknowledgment of God's unsurpassable greatness. Specifically, it is that mode of such acknowledgment whose attitudinal stance toward God is awed, reverential, and grateful adoration. Christians do not enact the liturgy in order to placate God, they do not enact the liturgy in order to keep themselves in God's good graces, they do not enact the liturgy in order to keep their ledgers on the positive side, they do not enact the liturgy in order to center themselves. They assemble to worship God. Facing God, they acknowledge God's unsurpassable greatness in a stance of awed, reverential, and grateful adoration.

If this is correct, then the understanding of God implicit in the Christian liturgy as a whole is, obviously, that of God as having an unsurpassable excellence of such a sort as to make it appropriate for us to adore God in a stance of awe, reverence, and gratitude. "Great is the Lord, and greatly to be praised." So let us turn now to that understanding of God.

---

3. I judge that there is something to be said in favor of identifying *trust* as a fourth component of that distinctive type of adoration that constitutes Christian worship.

What the Liturgy Says about God's Excellence

To describe God as being of unsurpassable excellence is formulaic. Many religious people would describe God as being of unsurpassable excellence; but when we ask them what it is about God that makes God of unsurpassable excellence, we get many different answers. My project here is not to offer up my own personal account of what it is about God that grounds God's unsurpassable excellence; my project is to make explicit the understanding implicit in the liturgy.

Notice the locution I used: "what it is about God that grounds God's unsurpassable excellence." Excellence does not just settle on things willy-nilly. Always there is something *about* the thing that gives it its excellence, some property that accounts for its excellence. It makes no sense to claim that a certain piano sonata is a fine sonata but that there is nothing about it that makes it fine, that it's just fine, period.

As to what excellence itself is, a property that certain things have on account of some property they possess or some action they perform, that is mysterious, deeply mysterious. To the best of my knowledge, no philosopher has succeeded in explaining it; I count myself among those. Philosophers have tried to formulate illuminating generalizations about instances of excellence. For example, philosophers of a certain utilitarian stripe have claimed that human wellbeing is the only intrinsically good thing, that anything else that's good is good by virtue of being instrumental to human wellbeing. Quite obviously that does not tell us what it is for wellbeing itself to be *good;* it does not tell us what goodness *is.* Robert Adams, in his book *Finite and Infinite Goods,* says that "things are excellent insofar as they resemble or imitate God," who is the non-derivatively and paradigmatically excellent being.[4] But that tells us neither what it is for God to be excellent, nor what it is for something other than God to be excellent; it does not tell us what excellence *is.* What it does instead is specify the conditions under which things other than God are excellent.

Our discussion here, as to what it is that grounds God's unsurpassable excellence, could be organized in many different ways. Let me organize it in terms of the three components of the attitudinal stance of Christian worship that I have identified: awe, reverence, and gratitude. Let's begin with awe.

---

4. Robert Adams, *Finite and Infinite Goods* (Oxford: Oxford University Press, 1999), p. 28.

Awe of God for God's Unsurpassable Glory

What is it about God to which awe is especially appropriate as a response? God's unsurpassable *glory*, I would say. We respond to our apprehension of God's unsurpassable glory with the attitudinal stance of awe, along, of course, with the action of *ascribing* glory to God. When I use the phrase "ascribing glory to God" I have in mind various passages in the Psalms, for example, Psalm 96:7: "Ascribe to the Lord, O families of the peoples, ascribe to the Lord glory."[5]

The theme of God's glory, and the counterpart theme of ascribing glory to God, receives explicit verbal expression in all Christian liturgies, if nowhere else, then at least in the conclusion of the Lord's Prayer and in a good many of the psalms and hymns that are sung, chanted, or declaimed. In the Orthodox liturgy, explicit verbal expression of the theme of God's glory is not just present but pervasive and prominent. Let me cite just three examples. In concluding the opening prayers of the liturgy the priest says, "Lord, our God, whose power we cannot conceive and whose glory we cannot comprehend" (13). Immediately before the Gospel procession he says, speaking now more expansively:

> Master and Lord, our God, who have instituted in heaven the orders and hosts of angels and archangels to minister to your glory, grant that we may be accompanied into your sanctuary by the holy angels and together minister and glorify your goodness. For to you belong glory, honor, and worship. (21)

And in the Trisagion Hymn, part of which I quoted earlier, the people sing, "Glory to the Father, and to the Son, and to the Holy Spirit, now and ever, and for evermore" (25).

It would be a serious mistake, however, to look only to the words

---

5. Cf. Ps. 29:

> Ascribe to the LORD, O heavenly beings,
>   ascribe to the LORD glory and strength.
> Ascribe to the LORD the glory of his name;
>   worship the LORD in holy splendor. . . .
> The voice of the LORD is powerful,
>   The voice of the LORD is full of majesty.

See also Ps. 96:7-9.

of the liturgy for an expression of the attitudinal stance of awe. We also express awe by kneeling, or by standing in silence. And the architecture is, or can be, expressive of awe, as can the music and the two-dimensional visual art.

For you and me, glory is not a familiar concept. We don't use the idea much, not the idea of glory that occurs in the liturgy. The idea enters the liturgy from Christian Scripture, both Old and New Testaments, especially from the Psalms, where God's glory is a prominent theme. In our English translations of the Old Testament the term "glory" is usually the translation of the Hebrew word *kabod,* connoting honor, weight, heaviness, or, as we might say, *gravitas.* The Septuagint translated the Hebrew *kabod* with the Greek *doxa,* a word that connotes splendor. God's glory is God's splendor. The biblical writers think of glory as a property of God that is manifested or displayed in God's works; God's glory shines forth in God's works.

God's glory is manifested in God's works of creation and maintenance of creation: in their awesome immensity, their intricacy, their regularity, their diversity, their beauty. "The heavens are telling the glory of God," says the Psalmist, "and the firmament proclaims his handiwork" (Ps. 19:1). Paul picks up and adapts this declaration of the Psalmist in the opening chapter of his Letter to the Romans when he says, "Ever since the creation of the world God's eternal power and divine nature, invisible though they are, have been understood and seen through the things he has made."

The idea of God's glory as manifested in God's works comes to expression most elaborately in Psalm 145:3-6:

> Great is the LORD, and greatly to be praised;
> his greatness is unsearchable.
> One generation shall laud your works to another,
> and shall declare your mighty acts.
> On the glorious splendor of your majesty,
> and on your wondrous works, I will meditate.
> The might of your awesome deeds shall be proclaimed,
> and I will declare your greatness.

Greatness, glory, splendor, majesty, wondrous works, awesome deeds — a flurry of terms indicative of glory are crowded together in these few brief lines.

What is it about God that is manifested in God's works of creation and maintenance of creation that we find awesome? Wherein lies what might be called God's *creational glory?* Mainly in three attributes of God. First, God's creational glory is grounded in God's power. The Psalmist, in the Psalm just quoted, spoke of the might of God's awesome deeds; Paul spoke of God's eternal power. This immense, intricate, diverse, regular and beautiful cosmos is a manifestation of astounding power, awesome beyond comprehension; it's part of what makes God glorious.

Second, God's creational glory is grounded in God's wisdom. Over and over this comes to expression in the Psalms. After twenty-three verses of ecstatic celebration of the diversity of creation in Psalm 104 the Psalmist declares,

> O Lord, how manifold are your works!
>> In wisdom you have made them all;
>> the earth is full of your creatures. . . .
> May the glory of the Lord endure forever;
>> may the Lord rejoice in his works.[6]

Third, God's creational glory is grounded in God's maintenance of the creation-order, in God's fidelity to creation. This is implicit in the Psalmist's celebration of the diversity of creation in the Psalm just mentioned. God maintains the order of creation so that the sun rises and sets each day, so that the moon marks the seasons, so that clouds water the mountains, so that springs gush forth in the valleys giving drink to the wild animals, so that there are trees in which birds can find habitation, so that there is grass for cattle to eat and plants for people to use, and so forth, on and on.

When composing this chapter I discovered, to my surprise, that this theme of God's creational glory receives relatively little explicit verbal recognition in the ordinaries of the traditional Sunday morning liturgies. In

---

6. Cf. Prov. 3:19-20:

> The Lord by wisdom founded the earth;
>> by understanding he established the heavens;
> by his knowledge the deeps broke open,
>> and the clouds drop down the dew.

And cf. Ps. 92:5-6:

> How great are your works, O Lord!
>> Your thoughts are very deep!
> The dullard cannot know,
>> the stupid cannot understand this.

the ordinary of the Orthodox liturgy I find just three references to God's creational glory, each of them brief. At one point the priest says,

> Holy God, who dwell in your saints and are praised by the seraphim with the thrice-holy hymn, who are glorified by the cherubim and worshipped by all the powers of heaven; you who have brought all things to being from non-being, who have created man in your image and adorned him with all the gifts of your grace. (25)

Later he says,

> It is proper and right to praise, bless, glorify, thank, and worship you in all places of your dominion. . . . You have brought us from non-being into being. (45)

And at a later point he says:

> We give thanks to you, invisible king, who by your infinite power have created all things and in your great mercy have brought all things from non-being into being. (63)

Explicit references to God's creational glory are equally fugitive in the ordinary of the Episcopal liturgy; I find just two. Eucharistic Prayer C, in Rite Two for the Eucharist, begins,

> God of all power, Ruler of the universe, you are worthy of glory and praise. At your command all things came to be: the vast expanse of interstellar space, galaxies, suns, the planets in their courses, and this fragile earth, our island home. From the primal elements you brought forth the human race, and blessed us with memory, reason, and skill. (370)

And Eucharistic Prayer D, in the same rite, includes these lines:

> We acclaim you, holy Lord, glorious in power. Your mighty works reveal your wisdom and power. (373)

Why the relative paucity of explicit references in the ordinary of the Sunday liturgy to God's creational glory? Should we conclude that God's creational glory is only a minor component within the understanding of God implicit in the Christian liturgy? Surely not. All Christian liturgies include the singing of hymns and psalms; and all traditional liturgies, with the exception of the Orthodox, specify for each Sunday a Psalm for that Sunday to be sung, chanted, or said.[7] In these hymns and psalms God's creational glory is a prominent theme. So if we look beyond texts for the ordinary of the Sunday liturgy to actual enactments of the Christian liturgy, prominent in the understanding of God explicit in the liturgy as a whole will be that of God as possessing unsurpassable creational glory. But I have no explanation for the fact that the ordinary of the traditional Sunday liturgies is so chary of giving explicit verbal expression to God's creational glory.

In verse 14 of the first chapter of John's gospel we read, "And the Word became flesh and lived among us, and we have seen his glory, the glory as of a father's only son, full of grace and truth." God's glory is manifested not only in creation but also in the incarnation, and more generally, in God's work of reconciliation of which the incarnation was the central act. The church stands in awed admiration before what I shall call God's *redemptive glory.*

The recognition of God's glory manifested in the incarnation is anticipated in the Old Testament generally, and in the Psalms in particular, by the recognition of God's glory as manifested in God's kingship — God's rule over all humankind — and by the recognition of God's glory as manifested in God's election of Israel for God's redemptive purposes.

The recognition of God's glory as manifested in God's kingship receives vivid expression in Psalm 24:

> Lift up your heads, O gates!
>> and be lifted up, O ancient doors!
>> that the King of glory may come in.
> Who is the King of glory? . . .
>> The LORD of hosts,
>> he is the King of glory.

The recognition of God's glory as manifested in God's election of Israel receives recognition, among many other places, in Psalm 105:

7. The first two antiphons in the ordinary of the Orthodox liturgy use words taken from Psalm 103 and 146 respectively.

O give thanks to the LORD, call on his name,
  make known his deeds among the peoples!
Sing to him, sing praises to him;
  tell of all his wonderful works!
Glory in his holy name. . . .
The LORD our God is mindful of his covenant forever,
  of the word that he commanded for a thousand generations,
  the covenant that he made with Abraham.

[handwritten annotation: He misses the fact that G's glory is nothing less than G's presence which evokes/compells awe]

God's redemptive glory receives a great deal more explicit verbal recognition in the ordinary of traditional Sunday liturgies than does God's creational glory. Let me content myself with two examples. Here is part of the Second Antiphon in the Orthodox liturgy. The people are addressing God:

> Glory to the Father and to the Son and to the Holy Spirit, now, and ever, and for evermore. Only-begotten Son and Word of God, being immortal, you humbled yourself for our salvation, taking flesh by the holy mother of God and ever-virgin Mary; you became man without change, and were crucified, thereby destroying death by death; being one of the holy Trinity, together glorified with the Father and the Holy Spirit. (17-18)

And here is Eucharistic Prayer I from the Great Thanksgiving of Rite One of the Episcopal liturgy:

> All glory be to thee, almighty God, our heavenly father, for that thou, of thy tender mercy, didst give thine only Son Jesus Christ to suffer death upon the cross for our redemption. (334)

In summary: the understanding of God that is both implicit and explicit in our assembling to worship God is that God is unsurpassably great in creational and redemptive glory.

[handwritten annotation: No: God is present!]

Reverence of God for God's Unsurpassable Holiness

Our adoration of God combines reverence with awe. Whereas it is especially to the glory of God that we respond with awe, I suggest that it is especially to the *holiness* of God that we respond with reverence.

33

The theme of God's holiness is sounded explicitly over and over in all the traditional liturgies, most prominently, of course, in the *Sanctus*.[8] Already by the fourth century the *Sanctus* had been introduced into the Eucharistic Prayer. In our present-day liturgies it comes in a few slightly different versions. Here is the version found in the contemporary Catholic liturgy and in Rite Two of the Episcopal liturgy:

> Holy, holy, holy Lord, God of power and might,
> heaven and earth are full of your glory.
> > Hosanna in the highest.

The acclamation derives from the ecstatic song of the hosts of heaven that Isaiah heard when standing in the temple (Isa. 6:3):

> Holy, holy, holy is the LORD of hosts;
> the whole earth is full of his glory.

The song was heard again by John of Patmos in one of his trances:

> Holy, holy, holy, is the Lord God Almighty,
> who was and is and is to come!

But what is holiness? I mentioned that the idea of glory that occurs in the liturgy is not, for you and me, a familiar idea. The idea of holiness is even less familiar. So let's spend a bit of time trying to get hold of the idea.

In his *Religious Affections* Jonathan Edwards spends several pages discussing God's holiness. He first draws a distinction between what he calls God's *natural* attributes or perfections and God's *moral* attributes or perfections. God's natural attributes are those that constitute God's "greatness; such as his power, his knowledge whereby he knows all things, and his being eternal, from everlasting to everlasting, his omnipresence, and his awful and terrible majesty."[9] God's moral attributes are "those attributes which God exercises as a moral agent, or whereby the heart and will of

---

8. An exception: in the Orthodox liturgy, the theme of God's holiness receives more prominence in the Trisagion Hymn.

9. Jonathan Edwards, *Religious Affections* (New Haven: Yale University Press, 1959), p. 255.

God are good, right, and infinitely becoming, and lovely; such as his righteousness, truth, faithfulness and goodness" (255).

Having drawn this distinction between God's natural attributes and God's moral attributes, Edwards then declares that God's moral attributes or perfections together constitute God's holiness: the holiness of God, in "the sense in which the word is commonly, if not universally used concerning God in Scripture, is the same with the moral excellency of the divine nature, or his purity and beauty as a moral agent, comprehending all his moral perfections, his righteousness, faithfulness and goodness" (255). Edwards then says that it is not God's natural attributes but God's holiness that is the "objective ground of all holy affections" (256). "Holy persons, in the exercise of holy affections, . . . love God in the first place, for the beauty of his holiness or moral perfections, as being supremely amiable in itself. Not that the saints, in the exercise of gracious affections, do love God only for his holiness; all his attributes are amiable and glorious in their eyes. . . . But their love to God for his holiness is what is most fundamental and essential in their lives" (256).

In his *Church Dogmatics* Karl Barth develops an understanding of God's holiness that is similar to that of Edwards but yet significantly different. Rather than identifying a number of different moral excellences in God, declaring all of these moral excellences to be examples of God's holiness, and then leaving it there, as Edwards does, Barth regards each of God's moral perfections as a modifier of God's love — not as one among other instances of God's love but as a modifier of God's love. He then argues that God's love in all its modifications has the quality of grace; God's love always seeks to create fellowship with the creature who is alienated from God. God's gracious love is manifested, among other ways, in God's forgiveness. But there cannot be forgiveness, Barth argues, without judgment. It is this *judging* aspect of God's love, implicit in God's forgiveness, that constitutes God's holiness, God's forgiveness being, in turn, a manifestation of the gracious quality of God's love. The graciousness of God's love has a holy aspect, namely, its aspect of judgment.[10]

I am not happy with either of these accounts of holiness. On Edwards's account, we human beings find the holiness of God, once we recognize it, altogether attractive. Edwards speaks repeatedly of the beauty and sweetness of holiness. But recall Isaiah in the temple. Isaiah's response,

---

10. Barth's discussion of holiness is to be found in *Church Dogmatics,* Volume 2, Part 1, pp. 353ff.

upon hearing the *Sanctus* hymn sung by the host of heaven, was to recoil and burst out, "Woe is me! I am lost; for I am a man of unclean lips, and I live among a people of unclean lips; yet my eyes have seen the King, the LORD of hosts!" (6:5). One need not deny that Isaiah felt something of the attraction of which Edwards speaks; nonetheless, the prophet recoiled. The same episode shows up the deficiency of Barth's account. Isaiah does not recoil because he is a sinner faced with God's judgment; he recoils because he is unclean.

The question, of course, is whether you and I can make anything of this, given that the idea of being clean or unclean in the relevant sense is no longer part of how we think. My own view is that we can recover the ideas of *the clean* and *the unclean,* though they will never have for us the emotional loading that they had for people in other places and times.

To declare that something was unclean was to declare that it was defective or sullied in such a way that contact with it, or certain kinds of contact, would sully oneself. To prevent this happening, the unclean entity had to be cordoned off; or if not cordoned off, then shunned. The Israelites thought that women while menstruating were unclean; they thought that certain animals were unclean; and so forth. When we immerse ourselves in the details of their judgments about the unclean we find ourselves thoroughly bewildered; the sociologist Mary Douglas, in her famous book, *Purity and Danger,* tried to find some rationale in their judgments.[11] For our purposes here it doesn't matter whether she succeeded; indeed, it doesn't matter whether there *was* any rationale in their judgments. What matters is only the inference to be made about God's holiness from the examples they give of what is unclean. God's holiness is God's purity and perfection: God is in no way sullied, tainted, defiled, defective. God's holiness is God's transcendence, God's otherness. Not ontological transcendence — not transcendence of space and time. Transcendence of all blemishes, of all stains and taints, of all defilements, of all imperfections.

It is God's glory that evokes our awe; it is God's holiness that evokes our reverence. There can be glory of certain sorts without holiness, hence there can be awe without reverence.

The people living in Central Asia in the fourteenth century were in awe of Tamerlane, appropriately so, given his exploits of conquest. I have no idea whether anybody revered him; but we know enough about him to know that it would have been profoundly wrong to have done so. He

11. Mary Douglas, *Purity and Danger* (London: Routledge & Kegan Paul, 1966).

36

was an unspeakably cruel and wicked man, about as deeply stained and tainted as a human being can be. Our worship of God combines the attitudinal stance of awe of God for God's glory with the attitudinal stance of reverence of God for God's holiness.

Gratitude to God for God's Unsurpassable Love

The adoration of God definitive of Christian worship includes, so I suggested, gratitude along with awe and reverence. Christian worship of God is awed, reverential, and grateful adoration. I have suggested that awe is our response to God's glory and that reverence is our response to God's holiness. Gratitude, quite obviously, is our response to God's love for us, the form of love in question being love as care, that is, love that seeks to promote the flourishing of the other and to pay due respect to her for her worth.

Explicit acknowledgment of God's love for us pervades the Christian liturgy; it would be overkill to offer more than a few examples. In the contemporary Catholic liturgy the priest can choose from among three opening greetings. One is this: "The grace of our Lord Jesus Christ and the love of God and the fellowship of the Holy Spirit be with you all." In Rite Two of the Episcopal Church the priest says, at the beginning of Eucharistic Prayer A, "Holy and gracious Father: In your infinite love you made us for yourself; and, when we had fallen into sin and become subject to evil and death, you, in your mercy, sent Jesus Christ, your only and eternal Son, to share our human nature, to live and die as one of us, to reconcile us to you, the God and Father of all." And in the Orthodox liturgy, in a passage already quoted, the priest says, in concluding the opening prayers, "Lord, our God, whose power we cannot conceive and whose glory we cannot comprehend, whose mercy is boundless and love for man beyond words, look down upon us in compassion."

The understanding of God implicit in the attitudinal stance of gratitude is that of God as unsurpassably great in God's love for human beings.

Pulling It Together

Let me pull together what we have concluded, and then pose a question. My project in this chapter has been to identify the understanding of God implicit in the Christian liturgy as a whole — not in one or another liturgical act, not even in a certain type of liturgical act, but in the Christian liturgy as a whole. After taking note of a few of the many ways in which human beings have understood what they are doing when they engage in ritual activity, I affirmed the common view that Christians enact their liturgy in order to worship God. That raised the question, what is worship?

Worship, I concluded, is a particular mode of Godward acknowledgment of God's unsurpassable excellence; specifically, a person is worshipping God if her attitudinal stance, when engaging in Godward acknowledgment of God's unsurpassable excellence, is that of adoration. After noting that adoration has somewhat different content depending on the particular object of adoration and the agent's understanding of that object, I suggested that Christian adoration of God is awed, reverential, and grateful adoration of God. That led us to reflect on the understanding of God implicit in awe, reverence, and gratitude toward God. The conclusion I arrived at is that the understanding of God implicit in our worship of God, and often explicit, is that of God as unsurpassable in glory, holiness, and love.

My question is the following. I have affirmed the common view that the Christian liturgy as a whole is for the worship of God. But does that common view need to be qualified? Consider the liturgical actions of confession and intercession. In both cases we are facing Godward. But are we worshipping God when we confess that we have sinned? Are we worshipping God when we present our intercessions to God? In both cases we bring ourselves directly into the picture, in confession, ourselves as sinners, in intercession, ourselves as needy. When we bring ourselves directly into the picture in these ways, are we worshipping God?

And what about our acts of listening: listening to the opening greeting, to the absolution, to the closing benediction, to the reading of Scripture, and to the preaching of the sermon? Are these acts of worship on our part? Now and then one finds writers in the Lutheran and in the Reformed traditions using the category of *proclamation* rather than the category of *worship* as the overarching category for the Christian liturgy. That seems to me clearly to be going too far; singing a hymn of praise to God is not proclamation. But should we perhaps think of the Christian liturgy as a blend of worship and proclamation?

I would say that in confession and intercession we are worshipping God. Confessing to God that one has sinned against God is an implicit acknowledgment of God's holiness and authority. Recall once again Isaiah's

38

outburst in the temple: "I am a man of unclean lips." And interceding with God is an implicit acknowledgment of God's love and power. Thus both confession and intercession are acknowledgments of God's greatness. And both can and should be done in an attitude of awed, reverential, and grateful adoration. So yes, confession and intercession are worship.

A similar thing should be said concerning our listening to the sermon, to the benediction, and so forth. The presider's acts of pronouncing the absolution, preaching the sermon, pronouncing the benediction, are indeed acts of proclamation. In Chapter Eight I will argue that they are to be understood as God speaking by way of what the presider says. But I would say that our listening to these various forms of proclamation is, or should be, an act of worship on our part; our listening to proclamation in these various forms, in the context of enacting the liturgy as a whole, gives to our adoration of God its unique and distinctive Christian character. And should not the preaching of the sermon be understood as an act of worship on the part of the preacher — an adorational acknowledgment on his or her part of God's unsurpassable excellence?

These observations about the relation of proclamation to worship suggest a point made earlier, however. The fact that the Christian liturgy as a whole is for the worship of God does not imply that no liturgical act has any purpose other than that. In his First Letter to the Corinthians (chapter 14) St. Paul several times over makes the point that the assemblies are for "building up" the participants in the faith; he criticizes various things that were taking place in the Corinthian assemblies as not building up the participants. Though it is especially those actions which fit the description of *proclamation* that serve to build up the participants, surely the liturgy as a whole does have, or should have, that effect; it would be strange, indeed, if that were not the case. But being built up in the faith is not something that happens *in addition to* our worship of God; worshipping God in the way Christians do serves to build up the participants in the faith.

A Closing Observation

I close with the following observation. It is sometimes said that the Christian life as a whole is, or should be, worship. In this chapter I have assumed that that is not true. The Christian life as a whole is, or should be, an acknowledgment of who God is and of what God has done, is doing, and will do — an acknowledgment of God's unsurpassable excellence. But I have argued that worship has an orientation that sets it off from our work in the world, namely, a *Godward* orientation. Of course it is open to a writer to declare that he will use the word "worship" to cover everything that I call acknowledgment of who God is and of what God has done, is doing, and will do. But that leaves us needing some other word to pick out what I have called *worship* — to pick out that Godward acknowledgment of God's unsurpassable excellence whose attitudinal stance is adoration. And it has been my experience that those who declare that all of life is worship almost always downplay the importance of what I am calling *worship,* especially the importance of what I am calling *liturgical* worship. As to such downplaying, I made clear in the preceding chapter my agreement with von Allmen and Schmemann that in the enactment of the liturgy we have the clearest manifestation of what the church is — not the only manifestation, but the clearest.

A-hah!

The showman appears!

CHAPTER THREE

God as One Who Is Vulnerable

In this chapter I want to look at the liturgy as a whole from an angle different from that of the preceding chapter, and to elicit an understanding of God different from that elicited there. This understanding will be different in being *complementary,* not *incompatible.*

In the opening chapter I argued that those who participate in the liturgy are engaging in a scripted social practice for the worship of God. A social practice always has, for those who engage in it, a certain normative status. It may be a *good* thing for them to do, perhaps a *very* good thing, weightier in its excellence than most or all other good things that they could do. Or it may be a *bad* thing for them to do, perhaps a *very* bad thing. Then again, it might be something that is not merely a good thing for them to do but a good thing that they *ought* to do, a good thing that's obligatory for them to do, that they have a duty to do. If something is not merely a good thing to do but a good thing that is obligatory, then, if one fails to do it, one is guilty of wrongdoing. By contrast, if something is a good thing to do but not obligatory, one's failure to do it may well be regrettable, but it does not make one guilty of wrongdoing.

The Normative Status for the Church of Enacting Its Liturgy

What is the normative status for the church of engaging in the social practice of enacting its liturgy? Obviously this is a good thing for the church to do. But is it obligatory? In Rite One of the Episcopal Church the celebrant says, in opening The Great Thanksgiving, the following:

> It is very meet, right, and our bounden duty, that we should at all times, and in all places, give thanks unto thee, O Lord, holy Father, almighty, everlasting God. (333)

The point could not be stated more clearly: it is our *duty* to give thanks to God. I assume that the word "thanks" is functioning here as a synecdoche for worship in general: it is very meet, right, and our bounden duty to worship God.

In Rite Two of the Episcopal liturgy, the Great Prayer of Thanksgiving opens instead with the following words said by the celebrant:

> It is right, and a good and joyful thing, always and everywhere to give thanks to you, Father Almighty, Creator of heaven and earth. (361)

The rather ambiguous term "right" has been retained; but the term "bounden duty" has been removed and replaced by "a good and joyful thing." I think we can safely infer that those who composed Rite Two were uncomfortable with the idea that it is our duty to worship God; it is a good and joyful thing, indeed, but not a duty.

Which of these two rites is correct on this point? What is the normative status for the church of engaging in the social practice of enacting its liturgy? Recall from our first chapter Schmemann's claim that in enacting the liturgy the church *actualizes* itself, and the very similar claim by von Allmen that its enactment of the liturgy is an *epiphany* of the church. If these claims are correct, and I argued that they are, then surely it is too weak to say that it is a good and joyful thing for the church to assemble to enact the liturgy. Assembling to enact the liturgy is something the church *ought* to do; it is its bounden duty. Should it fail to do so, it would be guilty of wrongdoing.

I think here of certain passages in Scripture — Psalm 96, for example:

> Ascribe to the LORD, O families of the peoples,
>   ascribe to the LORD glory and strength!
> Ascribe to the LORD the glory due his name;
>   bring an offering, and come into his courts.
> Worship the LORD in holy array;
>   tremble before him, all the earth. (Ps. 96:7-9)

The sentences here are all in the imperative mood; our ascription of glory to the Lord is *due* his name, that is, due the Lord.

I dare say that a good many readers are like those who revised the Episcopal liturgy in being uncomfortable with the idea that, for the church, the normative status of engaging in the social practice of enacting its liturgy is that of *obligation*. They recall that we are commanded to love the Lord our God with all that is within us; and they think of obligation as incompatible with love. Love, so they think, pays no attention to duty and obligation, no attention to what is morally *required* of one. To treat God and neighbor as one is required to treat them is not to love God and neighbor.

I hold that this view assumes a mistaken idea of the love that Jesus enjoins on us in the two love commands. One is obligated to treat someone a certain way just in case one would wrong that person if one did not treat him or her that way. But surely the love that Jesus enjoins on us always sees to it that it does not wrong anyone. How could it not do this? Love incorporates obligation. Love typically goes beyond obligation; but love does *at least* what obligation requires.

Perhaps those who hold that obligation is incompatible with love also have a mistaken view of obligation. They note that we say to someone that he is obligated to do so-and-so when it appears to us that he is considering not doing so; saying to him that he is obligated then gives him a push in the right direction. But the person who loves God and neighbor doesn't need a push in the right direction.

It's true, indeed, that we typically say to someone that he is obligated to do so-and-so only when it appears that he is inclined not to do it. But from this it does not follow that when he *is* inclined to do it, he is not obligated to do so. One can be inclined to do what one is obligated to do; ideally, indeed, we would always be inclined to do what we are obligated to do. All that follows is that when someone is inclined to do something anyway, we don't ordinarily bother to say to him that he is obligated to do it.

The application of these points is that if one has the right understanding of love, of obligation, and of the relation of love to obligation, one will have no hesitation in saying that enacting its liturgy is not just a good thing for the church to do but obligatory.

Suppose that this understanding of the normative status for the church of enacting its liturgy is correct. Let me now move on to the understanding of God implicit in that normative status. What I said above is that if the church should fail to worship God, it would be guilty of wrongdoing. Now if one is guilty of wrongdoing, always there is someone whom one has wronged. So if the church is guilty of wrongdoing by virtue of failing to worship God, there would be someone whom it has wronged. Who would that be? God, obviously. The normative status for the church of enacting the liturgy presupposes that God is vulnerable to being wronged.

I realize that many will resist this conclusion; but I find the line of thought that I have laid out compelling. It's not just a good thing for the church to enact its liturgy for the worship of God; it's obligatory that it do so. But if it is obligatory that the church do so, then it wrongs someone if it fails to do that. Who could that be other than God? So God is vulnerable to being wronged. I see no way to evade this conclusion. We assemble to perform the liturgy in order to engage in awed, reverential, and grateful adoration of God who is of unsurpassable greatness. But the normative status for the church of enacting its liturgy implies that that same God is vulnerable to being wronged. This is deeply paradoxical. Or perhaps we should say that a dimension of God's unsurpassable greatness is that, by bringing into existence creatures who are capable of wronging him, God has made Godself vulnerable to being wronged.

I said "made Godself vulnerable." God did not have to make creatures who were capable of paying to him the awed, reverential, and grateful adoration that is due him and also capable of not doing so. God did make such creatures, however; and in doing so, God made Godself vulnerable.

Let's be clear about the sort of divine vulnerability presupposed by the normative status for the church of enacting its liturgy. Already in the early Church Fathers there were discussions on whether or not God is impassible, that is, whether or not God has negative emotions of any sort — anger, dismay, pity, and so forth. The Fathers knew, of course, that Scripture uses the language of negative emotions when speaking about God; the issue for them was how such language is to be interpreted. Until the nineteenth century most Christian theologians held that God is impassible. The near-universal view was that when the biblical writers apply negative emotion terms to God, they are to be understood as speaking figuratively.

Augustine argued, for example, that when Scripture speaks of God as pitying his human creatures, it should not be understood as attributing to God anything like the pity that we experience. Human pity brings "misery of heart"; but "who can sanely say that God is touched by any misery? With regard to pity, if you take away the compassion which involves a sharing of misery with whom you pity, so that there remains the peaceful goodness

44

of helping and freeing from misery, some kind of knowledge of the divine pity is suggested."[1] In short, the sort of love that we are to attribute to God is never the love of sympathy, of *Mitleiden,* in which one shares the suffering or negative emotions of the other person, but only the love of well-doing, of beneficence.

Anselm elaborates Augustine's idea in *Proslogion* 8. Addressing God, he says,

> How art Thou at once pitiful and impassible? For if Thou art impassible, Thou dost not suffer with man; if Thou does not suffer with man, Thy heart is not wretched by compassion with the wretched, which is the meaning of being pitiful. But if Thou are not pitiful, whence can the wretched gain so great comfort? How then art Thou, and art Thou not, pitiful, Lord, except that Thou art pitiful in respect of us, and not in respect of Thyself? Truly Thou art so in respect of our feeling, and art not in respect of Thine. For when Thou lookest upon us in our wretchedness we feel the effect of Thy pity. Thou feelest not the effect. And therefore Thou art pitiful, because Thou savest the wretched, and sparest the sinners who belong to Thee; and Thou art not pitiful, because Thou art touched by no fellow-suffering in that wretchedness.[2]

Already in the early Church Fathers there was also discussion of the closely related question of whether God suffers. In this case the focus of the discussion was on whether Jesus could have suffered on the cross without God also suffering. Almost all theologians until the nineteenth century argued that God is incapable of suffering. Any biblical language that suggests that God suffers must be interpreted figuratively.

When I say that the normative status for the church of enacting its liturgy presupposes that God is vulnerable, I do not mean to claim that God is vulnerable to suffering and negative emotions. I have argued in some essays that God is indeed vulnerable to such negative emotions as anger and pity,[3] or to something very much like those; however, I do not think that the liturgy as a whole commits us one way or the other on that

---

1. Quotations from J. K. Mozley, *The Impassible God* (Cambridge: Cambridge University Press, 1926), p. 105.

2. Anselm, *Proslogion* 8, trans. S. N. Deane (La Salle, IL: Open Court Press, 1964).

3. See the essays "Suffering Love" and "Is God Disturbed by What Transpires in Human Affairs?" in my *Inquiring about God: Selected Essays,* Volume 1, ed. Terence Cuneo (Cambridge: Cambridge University Press, 2010).

point. My claim as to what is presupposed by the normative status for the church of enacting its liturgy is that God is vulnerable to *being wronged*.

It's a good question whether one can be wronged, and realize that one has been wronged, without experiencing some negative emotion toward both the wrongdoer and the deed done; it is surely no accident that Scripture very often speaks of God as angered by our wrongdoing, as do our liturgies.[4] But whatever our answer to that question, being wronged is not identical with feeling some negative emotion toward the wrongdoer and the deed done. My claim here is only that the normative status for the church of enacting its liturgy presupposes that God is vulnerable to being wronged. If there are those who hold that God cannot be wronged, they will have to insist that the normative status for the church of enacting its liturgy is not what I have said it is.

The Understanding of God Implicit in Confession

Let us now move inside the liturgy and look at the act of confession. Confession of sin occurs in all traditional Christian liturgies. In its confession the church assumes or declares that God is the one against whom it has sinned; hence it is that we address our confession to God. Option B for the Penitential Rite in the contemporary Catholic liturgy begins with the priest declaring, "Lord, we have sinned against you." And one of the options for the prayer of confession in the Episcopal liturgy begins,

> Most merciful God,
> we confess that we have sinned against you
> in thought, word, and deed,
> by what we have done,
> and by what we have left undone. (331)

Though it is against God that we have sinned, our sin against God often takes the form of wronging our fellow human beings; usually that is made explicit in the text of the confession. We sin against God *by* wrong-

---

4. Cf. one of the prayers of confession in The Holy Eucharist: Rite One, of the Episcopal Church: "We acknowledge and bewail our manifold sins and wickedness, which we from time to time most grievously have committed, by thought, word, and deed, against thy divine Majesty, provoking most justly thy wrath and indignation against us."

ing our fellow human beings — though it should not be overlooked that we also sin against God by not paying to God the glory due God's name.

Now for the point: whereas the normative status for the church of enacting its liturgy presupposes that God is vulnerable to being wronged, the act of confession presupposes that God has in fact been wronged. For what else is sinning against God but wronging God? If there are those who hold that God cannot be wronged, and thus has not in fact been wronged, they will either have to insist that this part of the liturgy is deeply misguided and that they want nothing to do with it, or they will have to offer an analysis of this part of the liturgy according to which we are not really doing what we appear to be doing, namely, confessing to God that we have sinned against God.[5]

The fact that God has been wronged by God's human creatures is what lies behind the divine lament that we find here and there in the Old Testament prophets. Nowhere is the lament more poignant than in the prophet Micah:

> O my people, what have I done to you?
>> In what have I wearied you?
>>> Answer me!
> For I brought you up from the land of Egypt,
>> and redeemed you from the house of bondage;
> and I sent before you Moses, Aaron, and Miriam.
> O my people, remember what Balak king of Moab devised,
>> and what Balaam the son of Beor answered him,
>> and what happened from Shittim to Gilgal,
>>> that you may know the saving acts of the LORD. (Micah 6:3-5)

Our sin against God takes the form of depriving God of the obedience that is due God. The use of the word "obedience" here points to the fact

---

5. On the matter of God and Christ being wronged, this is what Calvin says when discussing the Eucharist: "We shall benefit very much from this Sacrament if this thought is impressed and engraved upon our minds: that none of the brethren can be injured, despised, rejected, abused, or in any way offended by us, without at the same time, injuring, despising, and abusing Christ by the wrongs we do" (*Institutes* IV.xvii.38, trans. Ford Lewis Battles [Philadelphia: Westminster Press, 1960], p. 1415). Allan Aubrey Boesak, in *Dare We Speak of Hope?* (Grand Rapids: William B. Eerdmans Publishing Company, 2014), quotes Dietrich Bonhoeffer as saying that to stand with the marginalized is "to stand with God in the hour of God's grieving" (p. 85).

that there is something else about God that is presupposed by the liturgical act of confession than what I have thus far pointed to, namely, that God has issued commands to us for the living of our lives. Our wronging God takes the form of disobeying God's commands. This is made explicit in the text for one of the prayers of confession in the Episcopal liturgy: "we have offended against they holy laws."[6] In general, to issue a legitimate command to someone who is capable both of obeying and not obeying is to make oneself vulnerable to being wronged by non-obedience. By issuing commands to us and giving us the freedom to obey or not obey, God made Godself vulnerable to being wronged by us.

It would be worth devoting one or more chapters to this aspect of the understanding of God that is implicit in the liturgy, namely, God as one who issues commands. But what I wish to highlight in this chapter is that God is implicitly understood in the Christian liturgy not only as vulnerable to being wronged but as having in fact been wronged. John Calvin's commentary on Genesis 9:5-6 is worth quoting in this regard: "This doctrine . . . is to be carefully observed, that no one can be injurious to his brother without wounding God himself. Were this doctrine deeply fixed in our minds, we should be much more reluctant than we are to inflict injuries."

The Understanding of God Implicit in Intercession

Let us move on to a different part of the liturgy, the intercessory prayers. In the Lord's Prayer we address God and say, "Hallowed be your name, your kingdom come, your will be done, on earth as it is in heaven. Give us this day our daily bread. . . ." In Chapter Seven I will discuss at considerable length how we should understand this reference to the coming of God's kingdom. What I wish to note in this chapter is that here in this prayer we also presuppose a certain sort of divine vulnerability.

The vulnerability is, once again, a vulnerability to being wronged. God's name is often not hallowed; thereby God is wronged. Accordingly, we pray that God's name will be hallowed, so that God will be delivered from this form of wronging. God's will is not done on earth as it is in heaven; thereby God is wronged. Accordingly, we pray that God's will be done on earth as in heaven, so that God will be delivered from this form of wronging.

---

6. These words occur in the second of the two optional prayers of confession in A Penitential Order: Rite One, p. 320.

When we pray for sustenance sufficient for the day, after having prayed from the coming of God's kingdom, a different note is struck. Here we are not just praying for right action on the part of human beings; down throughout history starvation has often been due to natural calamities: drought, flooding, hurricanes.

We would not pray for the coming of God's kingdom if the kingdom were already fully here; we do not pray that God may be triune, or omniscient, or omnipotent. Neither would we pray for sustenance sufficient for the day if such sustenance invariably and inevitably came our way. The conclusion seems inescapable that there is in reality some strange resistance to the coming of God's kingdom; this is the significance, for example, of Jesus casting out demons. Paul sometimes refers to this resistance with such words as "powers," "principalities," "authorities." That's what he is alluding to when he says about the last days, "Then comes the end, when Christ delivers the kingdom to God the Father after destroying every rule and every authority and power. For he must reign until he has put all his enemies under his feet" (1 Cor. 15:24-25). Part of the resistance to the coming of God's kingdom is, of course, to be located in us human beings: often we do not hallow God's name, often we do not do God's will, often we do not exercise authority responsibly. But Paul teaches that such wrongdoing on our part is often due not just to the waywardness of our wills but to the fact that we are in the grip of malign powers. In his Letter to the Romans Paul speaks of us as "enslaved."

We who are Christians do not doubt that God will overcome this resistance and that God's kingdom will someday be entirely here; we do not wonder whether things are out of God's control. Sometimes we say to a fellow human being "May your efforts succeed" when we feel confident that they will. But until God's kingdom has fully arrived, there is resistance. And what this implies, obviously, is that God is vulnerable to such resistance. Not vulnerable in the sense that God is in danger of being overcome by the resistance; vulnerable, rather, in the sense that God has allowed resistance that God will overcome.

The Understanding of God Implicit in Blessing God

Consider, last, the blessing of God that occurs in most liturgies. In the contemporary Catholic liturgy it occurs at the beginning of the Liturgy of the Eucharist, upon the Presentation of the Gifts. The blessing spoken by the priest is in the declarative mood; the people respond with a blessing in the optative mood.[7] It goes as follows:

> *Priest:* Blessed are you, Lord, God of all creation. Through your good-ness we have this bread to offer, which earth has given and human hands have made. It will become for us the bread of life.
> *All:* Blessed be God for ever.
> *Priest:* Blessed are you, Lord, God of all creation. Through your good-ness we have this wine to offer, fruit of the vine and work of human hands. It will become our spiritual drink.
> *All:* Blessed be God for ever.

In the Orthodox and the Episcopal liturgies, the blessing of God occurs at the opening of the liturgy and is in the optative mood. In the Orthodox liturgy the priest says:

> Blessed be the kingdom
> of the Father, and of the Son,
> and of the Holy Spirit,
> now, and ever, and for evermore. (9)

What it is to *bless* someone has long been a much-discussed topic. What was God doing when, after having created human beings, God blessed them and said, "Be fruitful and multiply, and fill the earth" (Gen. 1:28)? What was Jacob doing when, upon his deathbed, he blessed his twelve sons, "each with the blessing suitable to him" (Gen. 49:28)? What was the Psalmist enjoining himself to do when he said, "Bless the LORD, O my soul, and all that is within me, bless God's holy name" (Ps. 103:1)? What was Jesus doing when he blessed those who are persecuted for the sake of justice, saying of them, "theirs is the kingdom of heaven" (Matt. 5:10)? I propose taking from the literature dealing with this question only what seem to me the two main possibilities for what it is to bless God and God's kingdom.

One possibility is that blessing God and God's kingdom is no differ-ent from praising God and God's kingdom, or declaring them worthy of praise. That seems to me the natural interpretation when the blessing is

---

7. The text of the Catholic Mass that I will use is the one available on the Web site, "Order of Mass: Basic Texts for the Roman Catholic Eucharist," dated Oct. 20, 2011.

spoken in the declarative mood. When the priest, in the Catholic liturgy, says "Blessed are you, Lord, God of all creation," that seems to me no different from saying, "Praiseworthy, are you, Lord, God of all creation." When the Psalmist enjoins himself to bless the Lord, he is, of course, not thereby actually blessing the Lord but enjoining himself to do so. I think the most natural interpretation of what he is enjoining himself to do is to praise the Lord. That is, in fact, what he goes on to do in the verses that follow.

A blessing spoken in the optative mood, whether over human beings or God, seems to me to call for a different interpretation, however. When God blesses God's newly-created human creatures, God is speaking in the optative mood and saying, *May you flourish. May you be fruitful and multiply and fill the earth.* So too when the priest in the Orthodox liturgy says, "Blessed be the kingdom of the Father, and of the Son, and of the Holy Spirit," he is speaking in the optative mood and saying, *May the kingdom of the Triune God flourish.*

But does it make sense to say, *May the kingdom of the Triune God flourish?* Doesn't God flourish no matter what? The answer, surely, is that if it makes sense to *pray* for the full coming of the Kingdom, then it also makes sense to say, *May the kingdom of the Triune God flourish. May it come in its fullness.*

And now for the upshot of these remarks about blessing God. If our praying for the coming of God's kingdom in its fullness presupposes that God is vulnerable to resistance to the full coming of God's kingdom, then our blessing of God in the optative mood also presupposes that God is vulnerable to resistance to the full coming of the kingdom, and is in fact being resisted.

The Christian liturgy is deeply paradoxical in its implicit understanding of God. We assemble for awed, reverential, and grateful adoration of God, the understanding of God implicit in such adoration being that God is of unsurpassable greatness in glory, holiness, and love. But the normative status of our assembling, and of certain of the liturgical acts that we perform when we assemble, presupposes that God has not only made Godself vulnerable to being wronged and to being resisted in bringing about God's kingdom, but that God is in fact wronged and is in fact resisted. God is both of unsurpassable excellence and vulnerable. It would be a mistake to think of these as two aspects of God co-existing side by side. A component of God's unsurpassable excellence is that God has chosen and allowed Godself to be vulnerable in just these ways.

And what is the appropriate attitudinal response to our acknowledgment of this aspect of God's greatness? *Amazement,* I would say. Christian worship of God is awed, reverential, grateful, and amazed adoration of God. Of course, our amazement at God is not only amazement that God would allow Godself to be vulnerable to being wronged and resisted. It is amazement also at God's glory, God's holiness, and God's love.

CHAPTER FOUR

God as One Who Participates in Mutual Address

Every Christian liturgy gives explicit expression to a certain understanding of God. The liturgy for the Eucharist of the Episcopal Church opens with the celebrant blessing God by saying, "Blessed be God: Father, Son, and Holy Spirit." The blessing spoken by the celebrant makes explicit that God is understood as a Trinity.

But in every Christian liturgy there is also an understanding of God *implicit* in the liturgical acts that constitute the liturgy. Implicit in the opening act of the Episcopal liturgy is that God is one whom it is appropriate to bless. The celebrant doesn't *say* that God is one whom it is appropriate to bless; and so, of course, he or she doesn't explain what it is about God that makes it appropriate to bless God. He or she just blesses God. My project in this book is to make explicit and to articulate some aspects of the understanding of God *implicit* in the liturgy.

In Chapter Two we considered the understanding of God implicit in the Christian liturgy as a whole; God, we concluded, is implicitly understood as being of unsurpassable excellence, worthy of awed, reverential, and grateful adoration. In Chapter Three we considered the understanding of God implicit in the normative status for the church of enacting its liturgy, and in the acts of confession, intercession, and blessing; God, we concluded, is implicitly understood as vulnerable to being wronged and resisted. Let us now move on to the understanding of God implicit in some of the fundamental types of liturgical actions.

The Liturgical Actions of Addressing God

The liturgy for the Eucharist of the Episcopal Church has two rites. Both rites open with the blessing of God mentioned above, spoken by the priest, followed by the people blessing God's kingdom by saying, "And blessed be his kingdom, now and for ever." These blessings are followed immediately by a prayer addressed to God spoken by the celebrant. The text of the prayer is the same in the two rites except that the pronominal references to God are updated in Rite Two: "thee" is replaced by "you" and "thy" by "your." Let me quote the text of the prayer as it is found in Rite Two:

> Almighty God, to you all hearts are open, all desires known, and from you no secrets are hid: Cleanse the thoughts of our hearts by the inspiration of your Holy Spirit, that we may perfectly love you, and worthily magnify your holy Name; through Christ our Lord. (355)

The people respond, "Amen."

This opening prayer is the first occurrence of a type of action that recurs repeatedly in the Episcopal liturgy, as it does in all mainstream Christian liturgies: the people, the celebrant, or both together, address God with second-person pronouns. Let me give some other examples from Rite Two of the Episcopal liturgy.

On certain Sundays, the singing of the ancient hymn, "Glory to God in the Highest," follows immediately upon the opening prayer. The opening lines of the hymn go as follows:

> Glory to God in the highest,
>   and peace to his people on earth.
> Lord God, heavenly King,
> almighty God and Father,
>   we worship *you*, we give *you* thanks,
>   we praise *you* for *your* glory. (356)[1]

The opening sentence of the text for the confession of sin goes thus:

Most merciful God,
we confess that we have sinned against *you*

---

1. The emphasis on "you" and "your" in this and the passages that follow is mine.

in thought, word, and deed
by what we have done,
and by what we have left undone. (360)

Rite Two contains a number of options for the text of the intercessory prayers. The text of Form VI begins with the sentence "In peace, we pray to *you,* Lord God," and it concludes with this sentence:

Have mercy upon us, most merciful Father;
in *your* compassion forgive us our sins,
known and unknown,
things done and left undone;
and so uphold us by *your* Spirit
that we may live and serve *you* in newness of life,
to the honor and glory of *your* Name;
through Jesus Christ our Lord. (392-93)

Two versions of the text for the Great Thanksgiving at the beginning of Holy Communion begin with the words,

It is right, and a good and joyful thing, always and everywhere to give thanks to *you,* Father Almighty, Creator of heaven and earth. (361)

This is followed by the celebrant praying a preface proper for the day, after which the celebrant says:

Therefore we praise *you,* joining our voices with Angels and Archangels and with all the company of heaven. (362)

And one version of the text for the prayer said by celebrant and people after Communion goes as follows:

Eternal God, heavenly Father,
you have graciously accepted us as living members
of *your* Son our Savior Jesus Christ,
and *you* have fed us with spiritual food
and the Sacrament of his Body and Blood.
Send us now into the world in peace,
and grant us strength and courage

to love and serve *you*
with gladness and singleness of heart
through Christ our Lord. (365)

Over and over the celebrant and the people address God with second-person pronouns. One can, of course, address God without explicitly using second-person pronouns. One wonders, for example, whether the celebrant in opening the Episcopal liturgy is to be understood as addressing God when blessing God. Is there an implicit "you" between "be" and "God" in the sentence, "Blessed be God: Father, Son, and Holy Spirit"? The opening of the Catholic Liturgy of the Eucharist is a blessing of God spoken by the celebrant whose text does include a second-person pronoun referring to God, thus making it unambiguous that God is being addressed: "Blessed are you, Lord, God of all creation." Might it be that the opening blessing in the Episcopal liturgy should also be understood as addressed to God?

That would be possible except for the fact that the people respond by saying, "Blessed be his kingdom, now and forever" — not *your* kingdom, but *his* kingdom. God is spoken *about* in the opening blessing, not spoken *to*.

The hymn "Glory to God in the Highest" uses the second-person pronoun; so clearly it is addressed to God. But a good many other hymns speak of God without using a second-person pronoun, thereby often leaving it ambiguous as to whether or not they are addressed to God. One can, after all, praise someone without addressing him; we who are professors do this when writing recommendations for former students and friends.

I remarked above that acts of addressing God occur repeatedly in mainstream Christian liturgies: praise of God is addressed to God, thanksgiving for what God has done is addressed to God, confession of sin is addressed to God, intercessions are addressed to God, supplications of other sorts are addressed to God, and so forth, on and on. Let me now make a stronger claim. In all mainstream liturgies — Orthodox, Catholic, Episcopal, Lutheran, Reformed — not just *some* liturgical actions are acts of addressing God but *most* liturgical actions are of that type. This is not true, obviously, for the liturgies of those Protestants whose Sunday service is little more than sermon. And in no liturgy do all liturgical actions take the form of addressing God. Expressing one's attitudinal stance of awed, reverential, grateful, and amazed adoration by kneeling or bowing is not an instance of addressing God; so too, eating the bread and drinking the wine of the Eucharist are not instances of addressing God.

From the pervasiveness of acts of addressing God in the liturgy it follows that the understanding of God implicit in such acts is more pervasive in traditional liturgies than any other. Of course, every act of addressing God takes some particular form: the form of praise, the form of confession, the form of intercession, and so forth. And implicit in those particular forms of address to God will be some correspondingly particular understanding of God. But those particular understandings of God all presuppose the understanding of God implicit in the act as such of addressing God. That understanding, whatever it is, is pervasive and fundamental in the Christian liturgy.

Initial Observations on What It Is to Address Someone

To discern the understanding of God implicit in addressing God we need some understanding of what it is for one person to address another. In the next chapter I will have more to say on the matter; but let's begin our reflections here.

In some Episcopal parishes there is an annual blessing of the animals; *de facto* what this amounts to is a blessing of the parishioners' pets. People bring their pets into the churchyard and the priest blesses them. The *Book of Common Prayer* does not include a liturgy for this blessing of the animals; I don't know whether there is, nonetheless, a standard liturgy for this blessing or whether each parish devises its own liturgy.

I have never attended such a blessing of the animals. But I would not be surprised to learn that in blessing the animals the priest refers to them with the second-person pronoun "you." Naturally the priest does not expect that the creatures he refers to as "you" will realize that they are being blessed; the point of blessing them is not undermined by their not apprehending that they are being blessed. So too a priest might pronounce a blessing over someone in a permanent coma, referring to the person as "you," with no expectation that the person will apprehend that she is being blessed.

Dogs realize when one is speaking to them; goldfish do not. So when goldfish are presented for blessing and the priest refers to them as "you," is it correct English usage to say that he is addressing them? When the person who loves her goldfish refers to them as "You sweet little things," is it correct English usage to say that she is addressing them? When the priest blesses someone who is in a brain-dead coma, is it correct usage to say that he or she is addressing that human being? When someone, gazing at Pike's Peak, exclaims, "Oh, may you never lose your snowcap," is it correct English usage to say that he is addressing Pike's Peak? Are these cases in which someone or something is addressed even though the addressee is incapable of realizing that they are addressed, or are they cases in which, though someone or something is referred to as "you," the referent is not really addressed because it is incapable of realizing that it is addressed? Can one perform a speech act in which one refers to someone or something as "you" without addressing the being so referred to, or is the use of "you" an indicator of address?

I shall refrain from trying to answer this question. Let me instead introduce the term "strong address" for addressing someone in the expectation or hope that one's addressee will realize that they are being addressed. Whether all address is strong address, or whether there is also what one might call "weak address," is a question we need not try to answer. Henceforth, when I use the term "address" without qualification, it will be strong address that I have in mind.

What is it to strongly address someone? Among the many different sorts of speech acts that we perform, what is distinctive about strongly addressing someone?

I would say that for me to address Malchus is to perform a speech act with the aim or purpose that Malchus will attend to what I say, will grasp it, and will respond appropriately. Should I fail in my aim — should Malchus not attend to what I say, not grasp it, or not respond appropriately — I would still have addressed him even though my aim in doing so has not been achieved. It's possible for my attempt to address Malchus to go amiss in such a way that I do not succeed in addressing him; perhaps unwittingly I address someone else instead, or perhaps I don't address anyone at all. But success in addressing Malchus does not depend on success in my aim of Malchus attending to what I say, grasping it, and responding appropriately. What is the case is that my performing the act of addressing Malchus depends on having those acts on the part of Malchus as part of my aim and purpose.

When addressing Malchus I may want someone else whom I am not addressing, Martha, let us say, to overhear what I say to Malchus. I may want Martha to attend to and grasp what I say. So we have to distinguish between *having it as one's aim or purpose* that a certain person (or certain persons) will attend to, grasp, and respond appropriately to what one says, and *wanting* some person (or persons) to attend to and grasp what one says. Wanting one's action to have some effect does not turn that effect into one's purpose in performing the action. My purpose in addressing Malchus is not frustrated if for some reason Martha happens not to overhear what I say; my purpose in addressing Malchus is frustrated if Malchus does not attend to, grasp, and respond appropriately to what I say. Naturally there will be cases in which it is unclear whether it is one's aim and purpose that a certain person will attend to what one says, grasp it, and respond appropriately, or whether that person's attending to and grasping what one is saying is no more than something that one wants to happen.

If the purpose of my action is that Malchus attend to what I say, grasp it, and respond appropriately, then Malchus has been singled out in such a way that I can refer to him as "you" — whether or not I do in fact refer to him in that way. Referring to Malchus with the second-person pronoun, I can preface what I say with the words, "To you I say." If there is no one whom I can single out in this way, then there is no one whom I have addressed. If I want Martha merely to overhear what I say to Malchus, then I cannot, referring to her, preface what I say with the words "To you I say."

If I address Malchus, then I assume that he *can* attend to what I say and *can* grasp it. To save words, let me say that I assume that Malchus can *listen* to what I say. This is to stretch the ordinary use of the term "listen." Though we address others both in speech and writing, in ordinary usage it is only their response to the former that we describe as "listening."

Being incapable of listening comes in two forms. First, most entities are ontologically incapable of listening: mountains, numbers, stars, wetlands — none of them can listen. Accordingly, unless one is seriously confused one will never strongly address any of them. Second, among the entities that are ontologically capable of listening, some will be incapable of listening to one's address to them because they are not in a position to do so. They lack the requisite know-how, they are off at too great a distance, or whatever. I address someone in English on the assumption that she understands English. But as it turns out, she understands only Turkish, and so cannot grasp what I said. She cannot listen to it, cannot attend to and grasp it.

If I address Malchus, I not only assume that he is capable of listening to what I say; I also assume that he is capable of responding appropriately. And in the ordinary case, I not only assume that he is *capable* of doing these things; I address him in the expectation that he *will* listen, or that there's a good chance that he will, and in the expectation or hope that he *will* respond appropriately. My expectation that he will attend to and grasp what I say may, of course, not "pan out." He may be distracted and not notice that I am addressing him; or he may attend to what I am saying but find that he doesn't grasp it. So too, he may attend to and grasp what I say but not respond as I had expected or hoped; he may be completely unresponsive, or he may respond in a way that disappoints me.

To strongly address someone is to expect or hope for a certain reciprocity of orientation. I orient myself toward my addressee in the expectation that he will in turn orient himself toward me by listening, and in the expectation or hope that he will then also orient himself toward me by responding appropriately. Suppose that these expectations of mutuality are gratified. Suppose that I address Malchus as "you" and that he listens to what I say and responds appropriately. Or just suppose that he listens to what I say, whether or not he responds appropriately. Let me borrow the English title of Martin Buber's famous book and say that the combination of my addressing Malchus as "you" and his listening to what I said to him creates between us an I-thou relationship. This relationship is not an ontological fact about us; it is not in the nature of things that we stand in this relationship. The relationship is brought into existence, created, by my addressing him as "you" and by his listening. I can think about Malchus, I can talk about Malchus, I can shake hands with Malchus; none of those ways of engaging Malchus creates an I-thou relationship between the two of us. For that to happen, I have to address him as "you" and he has to listen, or he has to address me as "you" and I have to listen.

God as Listener

These general points concerning what it is to address someone apply to our addressing God. I hold that our liturgical acts of addressing God are acts of strong address. We address God with the aim or purpose that God will listen to what we say and in the hope or expectation that God will respond favorably. Earlier I stipulated that by describing someone as *listening* to what was said to him, I would mean *attending to and grasping* what was said to him. Let me now stipulate that by speaking of God as *hearing* what was said to God, I will mean *responding favorably* to what was said.

Implicit in our address to God is the assumption that God can listen to and hear what we say to God. More than that is implicit, however. We address God in the expectation that God *will* listen to what we say; and we do so with the desire that God will respond favorably to what we say. Accordingly, the understanding of God implicit in our liturgical actions of addressing God, no matter what the particular content of those acts, is that God is one who can and does listen to us and one who can respond favorably to what we say.[2] If God does in fact listen, then there is a reciprocity of orientation: we are oriented toward God in addressing God and God is oriented toward us in listening. This reciprocity of orientation brings into existence an I-thou relationship between God and us. God is a thou for us.

Apart from the understanding of God as unsurpassably great that is implicit in the liturgy as a whole, and the understanding of God as vulnerable that is implicit in the normative status for the church of enacting its liturgy, the understanding of God as one who can and does listen to us, and is capable of responding favorably to what we say, is more pervasive in traditional liturgies than is any other understanding of God, by virtue of the fact that most liturgical acts in those liturgies take the form of address to God. And it is more *fundamental* in those liturgies than any other understanding of God implicit in those acts. The understanding of God implicit in our liturgical act of confessing our sins to God and asking for God's forgiveness is that God can be wronged and can forgive. But more fundamental in the liturgy than the understanding of God implicit in this particular content of our address to God is the understanding of God implicit in the very act of addressing God.

Before proceeding farther, we must deal with an issue that arises when we apply the concept of *listening* to God that does not arise when we apply that concept to human beings. We human beings can fail to listen to what is said to us; we can fail to attend to it and grasp it. But God has cognizance of all that transpires in the world; God is omniscient. So it appears that God cannot fail to listen; it appears that God necessarily listens

---

2. David Kelsey, in *Eccentric Existence: A Theological Anthropology* (Louisville: Westminster John Knox Press, 2009), puts the point well: "Contemplative adoration of God expressed in Christian practices of prayer does not assume that the One addressed in prayer is distant and indifferent and must somehow be brought near and invoked to be attentive; rather they assume that the One addressed is already attentively with those who pray and yearns to be addressed by them. Correlatively, Christian practices of prayer do not assume that enactments of such practices somehow constrain God to respond in particular ways; rather, they assume God's radical freedom from their practices of prayer in order to respond in love for them that is unpredictably creative" (Volume 2, p. 753).

to what is said to God. Yet several times over in the prophetic literature of the Old Testament we find God declaring that God will not listen to Israel's rituals. "When you stretch out your hands, I will hide my eyes from you; even though you make many prayers, I will not listen; your hands are full of blood" (Isa. 1:15; cf. Jer. 11:11 and Amos 5:23).

One way of dealing with the problem here would be to treat it as a purely verbal matter: the meaning I have stipulated for my use of the word "listen" is different from what the word means in these passages in English translations of the Old Testament; perhaps in these passages it is synonymous with what I mean by "listens and hears."

I judge that this is not the best resolution of the problem. Quite clearly it was the view of the biblical writers that God's response to the prayers of God's faithful people is not mere cognizance of those prayers, on a par, say, with cognizance of what is going on inside some volcano. The Psalms speak of God as *bowing down* to listen to us; they do not speak of God as bowing down to take cognizance of what is going on within some volcano. This indicates a mode of attention that goes beyond mere cognizance, a mode of attention that God is free to grant or not grant. God's listening to what we say to God is not mere cognizance of what we say.

My claim that, apart from the understanding of God as unsurpassably great and as vulnerable that is implicit in the liturgy as a whole and in its normative status, the implicit understanding of God that is most pervasive and fundamental in traditional liturgies is that of God as listener, may well take a good many readers by surprise. In a half-conscious way we all know that it's true. Many of those not familiar with the passages from the Episcopal liturgy that I quoted will know of similar passages from other traditional liturgies. But most of us have been schooled to think of God as agent. A good many have written about God speaking or revealing, myself included; very few have written about God as listening, my prior self again included. Indeed, I know of no theologian or philosopher who has written in a sustained way about God as listener. I have no interlocutors on this point.

When participating in the liturgy we are naturally more aware of the *content* of our address to God — praise, thanksgiving, petition, and so forth — than we are of its *basic structure,* namely, that whatever its content, it is addressed to God and presupposes God as listener. Add to this that liturgy is primarily sermon for many people. These factors conspire to make us overlook the fact that, apart from the understanding of God implicit in the liturgy as a whole and in its normative status, the understanding of God that is most pervasive and fundamental in the traditional liturgies is that of God as one who can and does listen to us and is capable of responding favorably to what we say.

God as Free to Respond Favorably

I said that when we address God in the liturgy, we do so in the expectation that God will listen and in the hope or desire that God will respond favorably. Sometimes the desire that God will respond favorably remains implicit; but rather often it is given liturgical expression. To our confession of sin we add, "Lord, have mercy." To our intercessions we add, "Lord, have mercy" or "Lord, hear our prayer." To our praise we add, "Receive our praise." Toward the end of Eucharistic Prayer II of the Episcopal liturgy the celebrant says, "Accept this our sacrifice of praise and thanksgiving" (342). Each of these gives expression to our desire that God will respond favorably to the content of that particular address.

I observed that the understanding of God implicit in the desire that God will respond favorably is that God is capable of responding favorably. These liturgical expressions of that desire indicate that something more precise should be said. They indicate that God is implicitly understood as *free* to respond as God wishes. God is not bound to respond in a way that we regard as favorable, nor, indeed, in any other way. A fundamental assumption of the Christian liturgy is that the liturgy is not a device for manipulating God. God cannot be manipulated. God is free, both to listen or not listen and to hear or not hear. I will have more to say about this in a subsequent chapter.

God as Speaker

In traditional liturgies, a good many of those actions of the people that do not consist of their addressing God consist of the people listening. In some free-church Protestant liturgies, almost all the actions of the people consist of listening, the main exception being the congregational singing — when that has not been usurped by praise bands.

To whom are the people listening? To the minister, obviously, the celebrant, the leader, the readers, the musicians. But is that all? In the Episcopal liturgy, at the conclusion of the first and second readings from

Scripture, the reader says, "This is the Word of the Lord." The reader introduces the reading from the gospel with the words, "The Holy Gospel of our Lord Jesus Christ," and concludes the reading with the words, "The Gospel of the Lord" (325-26). After the absolution following confession the celebrant says, "Hear the Word of God to all who truly turn to him." The celebrant then reads one of four prescribed biblical passages, one being the familiar John 3:16: "God so loved the world, that he gave his only-begotten Son, to the end that all that believe in him should not perish, but have everlasting life."

Said or assumed in each of these cases is that the people have been listening not just to the speaker but to what God said or says. The words used are noncommittal as to whether the people are to be understood as listening to what God *once said* or whether they are to be understood as listening to what God is saying to them *here and now* by way of the reading of some passage from Scripture.

J.-J. von Allmen, the Swiss Reformed liturgical scholar to whom I referred in my first chapter, is emphatic in saying that the listening of the people should be understood as listening to what God said or says. By way of the reading of Scripture, God addresses us — or as von Allmen puts it, "the Word of God is proclaimed by its reading."[3] "To read Scripture is to experience the paschal joy; the Lord reappears, He who is the Word, to tell us of His love and His will to teach us who He is and who we are, to summon us and give us life" (133). Von Allmen claims that this was the near-universal teaching of the church until the Calvinist reformation, when some Reformed theologians claimed that God addresses us not by way of the reading of Scripture but instead by way of preaching based on Scripture. Von Allmen calls this position "inadmissible" and "contrary to the whole of ancient Christian tradition" (132).

He goes on to argue that the reading of Scripture is one of three distinct ways in which God addresses us in the liturgy. God also addresses us in what he calls the "prophetic" proclamation of the Word, that is, in preaching. Von Allmen highlights two ways in which this mode of God's address is distinctive. First, "in the hands of God, the sermon is a basic means by which there takes place a direct prophetic intervention in the life of the faith and of the Church, with the object of consoling, setting to rights, reforming, questioning. It shows that the Word of God cannot

---

3. J.-J. von Allmen, *Worship: Its Theology and Practice* (London: Lutterworth Press, 1965), p. 132. Subsequent references to this volume will be made parenthetically in the text.

become the prisoner of the Church . . . but that it is always also external to the Church, a living force which strikes the Church from without" (143). Second, "preaching is not merely the sign of God's freedom, it also manifests man's freedom, since it is that phase of worship in which the preacher can bear witness to the truth and reality of what has been proclaimed by the reader of scripture. Thus it introduces into the service an element of witness-bearing. In so doing it expresses one of the deepest mysteries of the love of God: If God gives Himself to us, it is to enter into the depth of our being and invite us to disclose Him to the world, clothed with our flesh" (143).

The third mode of God's address to us in the liturgy is what von Allmen calls the "clerical" mode. What he has in mind is "those moments when, in the service, the minister, by means of a biblical formula, declares and gives to the people the *greeting,* the *absolution* and the *blessing* of the Lord" (138). A traditional greeting at the beginning of the service, one of three options in the contemporary Catholic liturgy, is the celebrant saying, "The grace and peace of God our Father and the Lord Jesus Christ be with you." Von Allmen interprets this as God greeting the people by way of the celebrant pronouncing these words.

In the present-day Catholic liturgy the celebrant, after the confession of sins, says, "May almighty God have mercy on us, forgive us our sins, and bring us to everlasting life." Von Allmen argues that this should not be interpreted as a prayer addressed to God, to the effect that God absolve the people of their sins, but as God's declaration, by way of what the celebrant says, that God does absolve these people of their sins. This interpretation is clearly correct for the formula for absolution that we find in Calvin's Strasbourg liturgy: "Let each one of you truly recognize himself to be a sinner and abase himself before God, trusting that the heavenly Father wills to be propitious to him in Jesus Christ. To all those who in this way repent and seek Jesus Christ as their Saviour I pronounce absolution in the name of the Father and of the Son and of the Holy Ghost" (quoted in von Allmen, 140).

The two rites of the Episcopal Church conclude with a blessing, as does the contemporary Catholic liturgy. One of the options for closing in the contemporary Catholic liturgy is the priest's saying, "May almighty God bless you, the Father, and the Son, and the Holy Spirit." The Orthodox liturgy also closes with a blessing: "May the blessing of the Lord and His mercy come upon us, by His grace and love, now, always, and for evermore."

In the traditional Reformed liturgy there were two options for the closing blessing, one coming from the Pentateuch and one from Paul's letters. The one from the Pentateuch, the so-called Aaronic blessing, was this:

The LORD bless you and keep you;
the LORD make his face to shine upon you, and be gracious to you;
the LORD lift up his countenance upon you, and give you peace.
   (Num. 6:24-25)

The one from Paul's letters was this:

The grace of the Lord Jesus Christ, the love of God, and the communion of the Holy Spirit be with all of you. (2 Cor. 13:13)

Von Allmen argues that all of these closing blessings should be understood not as prayers addressed to God, asking God to bless the people, but as God pronouncing God's blessing of the people by way of what the celebrant says.

Suppose that von Allmen is right about all this, as I think he is, that in listening to the reading of Scripture, the preaching of the sermon, the greeting, the absolution, and the blessing, the people are listening to God's address to them.[4] It goes without saying that the understanding of God implicit in the liturgical actions of the people's listening, so understood, is God as one who speaks.

Pulling the Two Implicit Understandings Together

Let me pull things together. In traditional liturgies, most of the liturgical actions take the form of the people addressing God; if von Allmen is right, many if not most of the others take the form of the people listening to God's address to them. The enactment of the liturgy is the site of mutual address and listening between God and the people. In the liturgy we are joined with God in a community of addressers and listeners.

Something stronger can and should be said. Not only is the enactment of the liturgy the site of mutual address and listening between God

---

4. In Chapter Eight I will state von Allmen's view on these matters somewhat more precisely than I am stating it here.

and the people. The enactment is *for* that mutual address and listening. The people enact the liturgy *in order that* mutual address and listening may take place; this contributes to giving our liturgical adoration of God its distinctive character. Enactments of the liturgy are by no means the only sites in which we address God; nor are they the only sites in which God addresses us. They are, however, the *principal* sites in which mutual address and listening between God and God's people take place.

It must at once be added that mutual address and listening between God and the people do not constitute the entirety of the liturgy: the congregants kneel, they sit in silence, they eat bread and drink wine, etc. And the celebrant addresses the people, the people address the celebrant, and members of the people address each other. But there can be no doubt that most of the liturgy consists of mutual address between God and the people.

An essay in liturgical systematic theology can begin from any aspect or component of the liturgy and proceed to articulate the understanding of God implicit or explicit in that aspect or component. But liturgical theology, at its most fundamental, will begin from the understanding of God implicit in worship as such, and it will move on from there to the understanding of God implicit in mutual address between God and the people.

In *Summa Theologiae* Aquinas began with God as the unconditioned condition of all that is not God. In the *Institutes* Calvin began with God as one who reveals himself in creation and Scripture. In *Church Dogmatics* Barth began with the Word of God. In each case, the beginning shaped the overall configuration of the theology that was developed. There are things to be said for each of these starting points. But our starting point is significantly different from any of those, and it will shape the overall configuration of our theological reflections. It already did so in the preceding two chapters.

Maimonides-Style Analysis

Here is as good a place as any to raise an issue that must be faced both by liturgical theology of all forms and by biblical theology of all forms. I have interpreted the liturgy as pervaded by acts of strong address to God; we address God in the expectation that God will listen to what we say and in the expectation or hope that God will respond appropriately.

Not everybody interprets those actions in that way, however. Some who participate in the liturgy believe that God is ontologically incapable of listening. A blend of philosophical and theological reflection, perhaps with some bits of modern science thrown in, has led them to believe that God is the Ground of Being, or something else along those lines. They regard it as theologically naive to believe or assume that God listens. So though they join with their fellow congregants in saying the words of the blessings, the thanksgivings, the confessions, the intercessions, they do not understand what is being done as addressing God in the expectation that God will listen to what is said and in the expectation or hope that God will respond appropriately.

I regard such participation in the liturgy as what earlier I called *deviant*. These people refuse to accept that description, however, since it presupposes an interpretation of the liturgy that they reject. They concede that the words of the liturgy are the sort of words one would naturally use if one did expect God to listen; and they realize that most of their fellow congregants do have that expectation. But they hold that linguistic appearances are, in this case, deceiving: no liturgical action consists of our addressing God in the expectation that God will listen and with the expectation or hope that God will respond appropriately.

Some go beyond merely rejecting an analysis of the sort that I have proposed and take the further step of proposing an alternative analysis of the actions of the liturgy according to which those actions do not presuppose what they regard as falsehoods. Invariably these alternative analyses involve regarding the language of the liturgy as highly symbolic or figurative. Others decline to take that next step. They are content to live in two worlds, the world of the enlightened intellect during the week, and the world of the liturgy on Sunday where they join their fellow congregants in uttering the words and performing the gestures of the liturgy.

Most of those who deny that God listens to us also deny that when we listen in the liturgy, we are listening to God's address to us. They believe that it is just as ontologically impossible for God to address us as it is for God to listen to us. So at this point, too, they contest my analysis of the liturgy. When we listen in the liturgy, we are listening to what the minister says, nothing more, or to what the reader says, nothing more.

The medieval Jewish theologian Moses Maimonides addressed his masterpiece, *The Guide of the Perplexed,* to Joseph, an erstwhile student of his. Joseph is a devout young Jew who reads Torah and prays the prayers of his Jewish tradition. But Joseph is also a bright and devoted student of philosophical theology. And this combination of activities, to both of which he is committed, leaves him deeply perplexed. The understanding of God arrived at in the philosophy classroom is profoundly different from that which appears to be implicit and explicit in Torah and in the prayers. In the classroom he has learned, for example, that "the description of God, may He be cherished and exalted, by means of negations is the correct description — a description that is not affected by an indulgence in facile language and does not imply any deficiency with respect to God in general or in any particular mode. On the other hand, if one describes Him by means of affirmations, one implies, as we have made clear, that He is associated with that which is not He and implies a deficiency in Him."[5] But Torah and the prayers are full of sentences ascribing positive terms to God.

So Joseph is "in a state of perplexity and confusion as to whether he should follow his intellect, renounce what he knew concerning the terms in question, and consequently consider that he has renounced the foundations of the Law. Or should he hold fast to his understanding of these terms and not let himself be drawn on together with his intellect, rather turning his back on it and moving away from it, while at the same time perceiving that he had brought loss to himself and harm to his religion. He would be left with those imaginary beliefs to which he owes his fear and difficulty and would not cease to suffer from heartache and great perplexity."[6]

The aim of Maimonides in *The Guide* is to alleviate Joseph's perplexity by showing how the terms ascribed to God in Torah and in the prayers can and should be interpreted so that what is said of God is consistent with what has been learned in the philosophy classroom. In Torah and in the prayers, for example, we find the positive terms "omnipotent," "omniscient," and "possessed of will" being applied to God. What we should understand as meant thereby is that God "is neither powerless nor ignorant nor inattentive nor negligent" — all negative concepts.[7]

Let me now speak of a *Maimonides-style analysis* of the liturgy. A Maimonides-style analysis of the liturgy claims, about some part of the liturgy, that we have good reasons — philosophical, theological, or whatever — for holding that what we seem to be doing in that part of the liturgy is not what we are in fact doing, since what we seem to be doing presupposes falsehoods. We seem to be addressing God in the expectation that God will

---

5. *Maimonides: The Guide of the Perplexed,* trans. Shlomo Pines (Chicago: University of Chicago Press, 1963), I.58, p. 134.

6. *Maimonides: The Guide of the Perplexed,* Introduction to Part I; pp. 5-6.

7. *Maimonides: The Guide of the Perplexed,* I.58, p. 136.

listen. But that's not what we are doing; our philosophico-theological re-flections have led us to conclude that it is ontologically impossible that God would listen. God is not that sort of being. A Maimonides-style analysis of some component of the liturgy may or may not go beyond such critique to propose an alternative way of understanding what we are saying and doing in this part of the liturgy, a way that does not collide with the conclusions to which we have been led by our philosophico-theological reflections.

A fully developed liturgical theology would have to take account of the various Maimonides-style analyses of the liturgy that are on offer. I will have to limit myself to taking account of a Maimonides-style analysis that challenges my claim that a good many of our liturgical actions are actions of addressing God, in the expectation that God will listen and in the expectation or hope that God will respond favorably. That will be our topic in Chapters Six and Seven.

CHAPTER FIVE

God as One Who Listens

In the preceding chapter I noted that the type of liturgical action most pervasive in the liturgy is that of addressing God; and I argued that the understanding of God implicit in such actions is God as one who listens and hears. So let us now reflect on God as listener. In Chapters Six and Seven we will reflect on God as one who hears, and in Chapter Eight, on God as one who speaks.

Many theologians and philosophers have thought and written about God as revealer. Some, myself included, have thought and written about God as speaker. To the best of my knowledge no one, my former self included, has thought and written systematically about God as one who listens. It is surprising that no liturgical theologian has written about God as listener; but so far as I know, none has. Given that there is no literature on God as listener, the scholar's customary practice of refining, deepening, correcting, and qualifying what others have said on the topic at hand is not available to us here. We are entering uncharted territory.

We can distinguish between the understanding of God's *nature* that is implicit in our addressing God, and the understanding of God's *disposition* toward us that is implicit. The understanding of God's *nature* is that God is one who is capable of listening to what we say and is free to do so or not to do so. The understanding of God's *disposition* toward us is that God is one who *does* listen. I will be saying something about each of these.

Locutions and Illocutions

In the preceding chapter we reflected on what it is to address someone. As preparation for our theological reflections on God as listener, let us now reflect on the pair, addressing someone and listening to someone's address to one. Recall that by listening to someone's address I mean attending to it and grasping what was said.

I am a partisan of the speech-act theory of speech. The theory is by now well-known; so let me confine myself to reminding the reader of the distinction that the theory draws between what J. L. Austin called *locutionary* acts and what he called *illocutionary* acts; this distinction will be of fundamental importance for my subsequent discussion.

An example of the distinction will suffice for our purposes here; no need to attempt definitions of these two types of acts. Consider the sentence "The sun is shining" and its standard meaning in the English language. Suppose I utter or write that sentence with that meaning in mind, and thereby assert that the sun is shining. My uttering or writing that sentence with that meaning in mind is a *locutionary* act; my asserting that the sun is shining is an *illocutionary* act.

I could perform the act of uttering or writing that sentence with that meaning in mind without thereby asserting that the sun is shining; I might, for example, utter or write the sentence in order to illustrate some point I wanted to make. (In fact I did exactly that when writing the preceding paragraph.) Conversely, I could assert that the sun is shining without uttering or writing that sentence with that meaning in mind; I could do so by uttering or writing a synonymous sentence from some language other than English. What these points show is that, in the case imagined, it was indeed two distinct acts that I performed, one being a locutionary act, the other, an illocutionary act.

My locutionary act is, in part, perceptible; someone can hear my utterance or observe my inscription of the sentence — though of course they cannot hear or see my doing so with that meaning in mind. My illocutionary act of making an assertion is entirely imperceptible. It's not a universal; it's a particular. But it's an imperceptible particular.

The relation between these two acts of mine, the locutionary and the illocutionary, is not merely that I performed them simultaneously, though indeed I did. Their relation is that I performed the illocutionary act *by* performing the locutionary act.

One way in which we perform one act by performing another is by doing something that causes a certain event. For example, I can perform the act of turning on the light by performing the act of flipping the switch; I do so when my action of flipping the switch *causes* the event of the light turning on.

The connection between my locutionary act and my illocutionary act is not causal; my locutionary act does not have as one of its causal powers that it brings about my illocutionary act. The connection is rather what I have called, in some of my writings, a *counting-as* connection. My performance of that locutionary act *counts as* my performance of that illocutionary act. The reason it counts as that is that there is a linguistic convention in effect, according to which my performance of that locutionary act counts as my performance of that illocutionary act. In various writings of mine I have developed a theory of what it is for one act to count as another;[1] for our purposes here it won't be necessary to get into that. Enough to note that my illocutionary act occurs outside the causal order. My performing that act was an exercise of non-causal agency on my part.

Now suppose that, addressing you, I perform the illocutionary act of saying, *look how beautiful the sky is today,* and that I do so by performing the locutionary act of uttering the English sentence "Look how beautiful the sky is today" with the meaning in mind that that sentence has in the English language. Then for you to listen to what I said to you — to attend to it and to grasp it — is for you to gain cognizance of my illocutionary act. Thereby the two of us are linked: this particular illocutionary act, of my asserting *look how beautiful the sky is today,* is an act to which I stand in the relation of performing it and to which you stand in the relation of listening to it.

That we human beings are capable of becoming linked in this way — capable of gaining cognizance of the illocutionary acts performed by our fellows, imperceptible particulars that lie outside the causal order, both those illocutionary acts addressed to us and those not addressed to us — is remarkable. That our gaining cognizance of such entities is something we do routinely goes beyond the remarkable; it's amazing.

The Normative Dimensions of Addressing and Listening

It happens not infrequently that we refrain from listening to what is said to us, or listen to just enough of it to know that we don't want to listen to any more of it. One reason for this is that we don't have time to listen, or judge it best not to take the time. E-mail messages addressed to me come flooding into my computer; I judge that I have more important things to

---

1. See especially Chapter 5 of my *Divine Discourse* (Cambridge: Cambridge University Press, 1995).

do than read through each and every one of them. There is nothing particularly revelatory of the nature of listening in this reason for refraining from listening; most things that we do take time.

Not so for another reason for refraining from listening to what someone says to one. Sometimes one person refuses to listen to what another is saying to her because she regards it as beneath her dignity to do so. Some years ago an American aunt of mine married a Dutchman and moved to The Hague. At first my aunt knew almost no one in the church they attended. Nonetheless, after a service she did what she was in the habit of doing back in the United States: she greeted the people around her. According to my aunt, one of the people she greeted, a well-dressed woman, drew herself up and, in a voice dripping with sarcasm, said — I translate from the Dutch — "I do not have the honor of knowing you." My aunt did not hear this as an invitation to become acquainted; she heard it as saying, "Who are you to be talking to me?" Of course, there was some irony in the fact that the woman had not only listened to what my aunt said but replied, though in such a way, indeed, as to signal that my aunt was not again to address her.

This same reason for refusing to listen to someone is rather often used as a reason for refusing to speak to someone. Mary refuses to speak to Matilda because she regards Matilda as so inferior to her as to make it inappropriate to speak to her, shameful, perhaps even wrong. Matilda is of a lower social class, an untouchable. Or she is one of those repulsive immigrants who managed to enter the country illegally. Or she has acted in an utterly despicable way. Whatever the reason, for Mary to speak to her would require ignoring the great discrepancy in perceived worth between herself and Matilda. It would amount to Mary treating Matilda as having more worth than she does have. She's not worth speaking to. An emergency of some sort may make it necessary for Mary to speak to Matilda; if she does, each party realizes that a certain equalizing has then occurred. In speaking to Matilda, be it under duress, Mary honors her, grudging and temporary though that honoring may be.

Sometimes it's for the opposite reason that one person refrains from addressing another. She regards the other as too far above her in worth or status for her to speak to him; she doesn't dare speak to him. Who is she, an untouchable, to address a member of the upper class? Who is she, a mere commoner, to address the king? It would be unthinkably presumptuous for her to do so.

Suppose, now, that the social conventions are broken. Suppose that the king addresses the commoner, speaks to her, speaks kindly to her.

The king has not been misled or deluded into thinking she is not a commoner, nor has he forgotten that he is king. Nonetheless, he treats her as someone worth speaking to. Thereby he honors her. Seen from his side, he has humbled himself; seen from her side, he has elevated her. "Who am I, O king, that you would speak to me?" she thinks. Other members of the royalty regard themselves as above speaking to her and regard her as beneath their speaking to; they don't approve of the social equalizing implicit in the king's action.

Suppose that the king not only speaks to her but invites her to speak to him. She does; and he listens. Thereby he treats her as someone worth listening to. He honors her. Seen from his side, he has once again humbled himself; seen from her side, he has once again elevated her. "Who am I, O king, that you would listen to me?" she thinks. Other members of the royalty regard themselves as above listening to her and regard her as beneath their listening to; they sternly disapprove of the king's action.

The combination of one person addressing another and the addressee listening to what the addresser says constitutes a mutual honoring. The speaker may be reluctant to treat his addressee as worth speaking to; the addressee may be reluctant to treat the speaker as worth listening to. But mutual recognition of dignity is built into the addressing/listening relationship.

Sometimes a person refuses to speak to another for a reason quite different from the two I have mentioned, lack of time and disparity of social status. Sometimes one person refuses to speak to another because he is deeply alienated from him. The young man has flouted the will of the father so seriously, or brought such shame on the family, that the father turns him out and refuses henceforth to speak to him. The brothers are so angry with each other that they refuse to speak to each other.

I once witnessed the following near-incredible piece of behavior. I was in the office of a philosophy department along with two other members of the department, one of whom was not on speaking terms with the other. The secretary of the department, who I'll call "Nancy" (not her real name), was seated at her desk. The person who was not on speaking terms with the other found herself in the position, nonetheless, of wanting to communicate something to him. What to do? She addressed the secretary and said, "Nancy, would you tell so-and-so that such-and-such?"

Just as it often happens that one person is not on speaking terms with another, so too it sometimes happens that one person is not on listening terms with another. If the latter person says something orally to the former, she covers her ears. If the latter writes a letter to the former and the former discerns who wrote the letter, she tears it up without reading it.

What these examples point to is that both addressing and listening presuppose a certain degree of non-alienation from the other, a certain degree of toleration, if not harmony. One person may be intensely angry with another. But if he nonetheless speaks to her, even if only to express his anger, his alienation is not complete; it remains less than it might be. Or if he nonetheless listens to her, then too his alienation is less than complete. This is inherent in the very structure of addressing someone and in the very structure of listening to what someone says to one.

Being Astonished That God Would Listen

It's astonishing that God would listen to what we say to God. God is the creator and sustainer of our incredibly vast and intricate universe with its astounding diversity and order; you and I are mere specks within this universe. Why would God bother to listen to what we say to God? Time is not an issue. God has all the time in the world. But given the enormously important things that God has to do as creator and sustainer of the universe — uphold the inconceivably vast starry heavens, preserve the intricate interplay of subatomic particles, keep the proteins in the bodies of animals working properly, just to mention three things — why would God bother to listen to us? Indeed, why would God have bothered to make creatures who *can* speak to God and to whom God then *can* listen? Recall the words of the Psalmist:

> When I look at your heavens, the work of your fingers,
>   the moon and the stars that you have established;
> what are human beings that you are mindful of them,
>   mortals that you care for them? (8:3-4)

Angels, they might have something to say to God that's worth God's attention. But we human beings? That the creator and sustainer of the universe would find it worthwhile to listen to us is utterly astonishing. Evidently God places great store in listening to what we say to God; otherwise, why would God bother, given all that God has to do as creator and sustainer?

Our order of discussion has been from creatures to God; to understand what is involved in our addressing God and in God listening to what we say to God, we looked at what it is to address a fellow human being and what it is for her to listen to what we say to her. The order of things is the opposite of the order of our discussion. The order of things is that the God who is capable of listening to speech acts created beings who are also capable of such listening, creatures who image God in their capacity for such listening. In listening to speech acts we image what God does. To bear the image of God is to be capable of attending to and grasping speech acts.

To look more deeply into what it is for God to listen to what we say to God is to be yet more astonished that God would do such a thing. By listening to our praise, our thanksgivings, our intercessions, our blessings, our confessions, God links Godself with us. The very same speech act that we address to God is the one that God listens to. God is of unsurpassable greatness. Our speech act is a puny, transitory, circumscribed, and defective thing. By listening to what we say to God, the unsurpassably great God brings it about that this puny, defective act of ours becomes a link between us. This is astonishing.

There is something yet more astonishing in the fact that God listens to us. God is high and mighty, exalted above all the hosts of heaven. We are creatures of the earth, from dust and to dust. Yet God listens to us. To do so is to treat us as worth listening to, to honor us, to pay us the honor of listening to us. "Who are we, O God, that you would listen to us?" Puny though we are, God does not regard it as beneath God's dignity to listen to us. Seen from God's side, God humbles Godself; seen from our side, God elevates us.

Recall the hymn to Christ in Philippians 2:

> Though he was in the form of God,
>   [he] did not regard equality with God
>   as something to be exploited
> but emptied himself
>   taking the form of a slave,
>   being born in human likeness.
> And being found in human form,
>   he humbled himself
>   and became obedient to the point of death —
>   even death on a cross.

In humbling himself by taking on our nature, Christ exalted us: we now have the dignity of having the same nature as Christ.

I submit that the humbling and exaltation that occur when God listens to what we say to God should be seen as foreshadowing the humbling and exaltation that occurred at the incarnation. The Psalmist was aware of the former humbling. Psalm 86 opens with the plea, "Incline your ear, O LORD, and answer me,/for I am poor and needy."[2] In Psalm 138:6 he says, "Though the LORD is high, he regards the lowly."

In *The Personhood of God: Biblical Theology, Human Faith and the Divine Image,* the Jewish writer Yochanan Muffs says this:

> One should not take this display of interest [by God for human beings] too lightly, for the true turning of God toward man was a total revolution in the religious world of the ancient Near East. The gods of Babylonia were completely dependent on nature and fate. Their major interest was themselves: the satisfaction of their needs, their hates, and their loves. The gods of Babylonia were not interested in the private destiny of man. To satisfy their physical needs, they turned to the king.[3]

God's listening to what we say to God obviously presupposes that God takes an interest in us. What I have been arguing is that God's interest in us takes an utterly astonishing form. It takes the form of the creator and sustainer of the universe treating us as being worthy of listening to, thereby honoring us. It takes the form of the one who is exalted above all the hosts of heaven humbling himself and simultaneously elevating us, creatures of dust. It takes the form of the one who is unsurpassably great linking himself to us by listening to that very same puny, transitory, circumscribed, defective act that we performed, namely, the speech act that we addressed to God.

Is It Presumptuous to Address God?

But is it not presumption of mind-blowing proportion to address God in the conviction or expectation that God will listen? Commoners don't dare address the king; they are much too lowly. Beholding the king when in his

---

2. The metaphor of God inclining to listen also occurs in Pss. 40:1, 71:2, 88:2, and 102:2.

3. Yochanan Muffs, *The Personhood of God: Biblical Theology, Human Faith, and the Divine Image* (Woodstock, VT: Jewish Lights, 2005), p. 14.

presence, that's something they dare to do; praising and obeying him when out of his presence, that's also something they dare to do. But they don't dare address him. Who do we Christians (and Jews and Muslims) think we are, addressing God when enacting our liturgies?

And who do we think God is, if we think God will listen to us? Should the commoner get it into his head to address the king, the king won't listen; his status is too elevated, and he has more important things to do. Doesn't our action of addressing God, in the conviction or expectation that God will listen, imply a shockingly low view of God and/or a shockingly high view of ourselves?

One reason the church believes it is not presumptuous for us to address God, in the expectation that God will listen, is that it believes that the Psalms, included in its sacred scripture, are not just a record of some ancient Jewish prayers but a gift of God to the Jews down through the ages and then also to the church, to be used by the church both as storehouse and model for its own prayers.

The great majority of the Psalms take the form of address to God. The church takes the words of these Psalms onto its own lips, not to recite them as one might recite some lyric poem but so as to address God thereby. Our locutionary act of taking onto our lips the words of the ancient Psalm, often with considerable change of meaning, counts as our illocutionary act of here and now addressing God.

Over and over, dozens of times, sometimes with great urgency, sometimes with evident confidence, sometimes in worried tones, the Psalmist says: "hear my prayer" (4:1), "hear, O LORD, answer me" (27:7), "incline your ear" (17:6), "make haste to answer me" (143:7), "hear my voice" (64:1), "answer me when I call" (4:1), "give ear to my cry" (39:12), "let the words of my mouth be acceptable to you" (19:14). The opening of Psalm 55 is especially emphatic:

> Give ear to my prayer, O God;
>> do not hide yourself from my supplication.
> Attend to me, and answer me.

I said that the church, in enacting its liturgies, addresses God in the confidence or expectation that God will listen. These cries of the Psalmist, taken by the church onto its own lips, might be thought to belie this claim. Rather than addressing God in the confidence or expectation that God will listen, is not the Psalmist, in worried tones, beseeching God to listen?

That cannot be the right interpretation. The Psalmist's cry is not addressed to some angels, asking them to get God to listen. The Psalmist's cry is addressed to God. Why cry to God if you don't think God will listen? Or to speak more cautiously: if you don't think either that God will listen or that there is a good chance that God will listen? The Psalmist's cry is not a cry for God to listen to the Psalmist's praise, thanksgiving, intercession and confession. He assumes that God will listen. It's a cry for God to hear.

Another reason the church believes that it is not presumptuous for us to address God is that it believes that God has invited us to do so. Suppose that the king invites the commoner to address him; then it is not presumption on the part of the commoner to address the king but grateful acceptance of the king's gracious offer. The gospel of Matthew reports Jesus as saying to his disciples, "Pray in this way," whereupon Jesus offers the paradigmatic prayer (Matthew 6:9). The church interprets Jesus' teaching his disciples how to pray as God's word to the church; we are to pray as Christ taught his disciples to pray. Addressing the creator and sustainer of the universe would indeed be presumptuous on our part were it not for the fact that the creator and sustainer of the universe has invited us to do exactly that.

Isn't It Pointless to Address God?

But isn't it pointless to address God? God knows our every thought. So when we express our thoughts in uttered or written sentences, what more is there for God to know than God already knows, other than the fact, surely insignificant from God's perspective, that we do so in English rather than, say, in Dutch or Turkish?

The idea implicit in this query is that to speak is to express one's thoughts in some physical medium, interpretation then being understood as moving in the reverse direction, from physical medium to thought expressed. The combination of expressing one's thoughts in some physical medium, and one's addressee inferring from those physical media the thoughts expressed, constitutes the communication or transmission of thoughts from speaker to addressee. This expression theory of speech, with its correlative theory of interpretation, was common among the Romantics.

We human beings have no other way of knowing the thoughts of our fellow human beings than by their expressing those thoughts in some physical medium and our interpreting that medium for the thoughts expressed. But God already knows our thoughts, before we express them and whether or not we express them. So what could possibly be the point of God inviting us to address God?

Speech-act theory helps us to see that the question rests on mistaken assumptions. To speak is not to express or manifest some mental state but to perform some illocutionary act. One's performance of some illocutionary act typically does indicate that one has certain mental states; but the act itself is not to be identified with such indication. Though my promising to do something usually indicates that I intend to do it, I can promise to do something without intending to do it, and I can intend to do it, and indicate that I intend to do it, without promising to do it. When I promise to do something I make myself obligated to do it; merely expressing my intention to do something does not make me obligated to do it. So too, when I assert something, my doing so usually indicates that I believe the proposition asserted; but I can assert something without believing it, and I can indicate that I believe it without asserting it.

In short, the fact that God knows our innermost thoughts does not render it pointless for us to address God. Addressing God is not the same as expressing a thought.

God's Listening Is Not Unconditional

I have argued that when we assemble to enact the liturgy, we follow the model of the Psalmist and address God in the confidence or expectation that God will listen. But in an earlier chapter I pointed to those passages in the Old Testament prophets in which God declares that God will not listen to Israel's rituals. These passages indicate that God's listening is not unconditional. Not only is God free to listen or not listen to our address to him. Sometimes God does in fact not listen. God does not listen no matter what.

Earlier in this chapter we took note of the fact that the alienation of one person from another may be so severe that the former refuses to speak to the latter; she is not on speaking terms with him. Alienation may also result in one person refusing to listen to the other; she's not on listening terms with him. Evidently it's possible for God to be so alienated from us as not to be on listening terms with us. God turns a deaf ear to what we say — not just a deaf ear to our cry to respond favorably to our intercessions, but a deaf ear to those intercessions themselves.[4] It is especially when one stands outside the liturgy that this possibility looms up. That's what the Old Testament prophets did: stood outside Israel's rituals and declared that God was not listening. Let me quote once again the well-known passage from the prophet Amos; God is the speaker:

> I hate, I despise your festivals
>   and I take no delight in your solemn assemblies.
> Even though you offer me your burnt offerings and grain offerings,
>   I will not accept them;
> and the offerings of well-being of your fatted animals
>   I will not look upon.
> Take away from me the noise of your songs;
>   I will not listen to the melody of your harps. (Amos 5:21-23)

What was it that so deeply alienated God from Israel that God refused to take note of their rituals? After Amos had pronounced judgment on the surrounding peoples of Damascus, Gaza, Tyre, Edom, Ammon, and Moab for their transgressions, the prophet turned his withering gaze on Israel and Judah and pronounced judgment on them for their transgressions, vividly described: "you trample on the poor," "you take from the poor levies of grain," "you push aside the needy in the gate," "you turn justice to wormwood." It was the rampant injustice in Israel and Judah that caused God's alienation. The alienation was so deep that God not only brought judgment on them but paid no attention to what they said and did in their rituals.

Isaiah makes the same point as Amos: it's the rampant injustice within Israel that has caused God's alienation. "Even though you make many prayers, I will not listen; your hands are full of blood.... Cease to do evil, learn to do good; seek justice" (1:15-17). In the book of Jeremiah it is Israel's idolatry rather than her injustice that has brought about God's alienation: "They have gone after other gods to serve them.... Therefore, thus says the LORD, Behold, I am bringing evil upon them which they cannot escape; though they cry to me, I will not listen to them" (11:10-11).

These passages obviously tell us something of fundamental importance about God; but they also tell us something of fundamental impor-

---

4. Recall that, in the preceding chapter, I distinguished between God having cognizance of what we say and God attending to what we say.

tance about Jewish and Christian liturgy. As I noted in Chapter Two, one infers from some of the things that Amos and other Old Testament prophets said that Israel and Judah thought of participation in its liturgy as *pleasing* God; the people assemble to offer sacrifices, sing songs, play instruments, recite prayers, and so forth, on the assumption that God likes that sort of thing. It's not clear from what the prophets say whether the people thought of this as compensating for God's displeasure over what they were doing in their everyday lives, or whether they thought that God was indifferent to what they did in their everyday lives but very much enjoyed their rituals. Either way, they assumed that the idolatry and rampant injustice present in their lives would not detract from the delight God gets from the songs they sing and the sacrifices they make in their solemn assemblies.

The prophets reject out of hand this understanding of the liturgy. In Chapter Two I introduced the idea of a *deviant* participation in the liturgy; I said that those who participate in the Christian liturgy for some reason other than to worship the Christian God are engaged in a deviant participation. What we learn from the prophets is that even if we faithfully follow the verbal and behavioral script for the liturgy, our participation may nonetheless be so deviant that God refuses to listen to us when we address God.

What is especially striking in the prophetic denunciations is that it was not what the members of Israel and Judah were doing in the liturgy itself that made their enactment unacceptably deviant but what they were doing in their lives *outside* the liturgy. Let me explain what I take to be the underlying idea here. I said that the Christian life as a whole is to be a life in which one acknowledges who God is and what God has done, is doing, and will do, namely, a being of unsurpassable excellence who is worthy of awed, reverential, grateful, and amazed adoration; and I suggested that worship is a special mode of such acknowledgment. Now imagine a subject of some king who bows down to the king and praises him when in the king's presence, but who puts the king completely out of mind when he is not in the king's presence — pays as little attention as possible to whatever rules and regulations the king hands down, feels more loyalty to some foreign monarch than he does to his king, and so forth. What this person does when out of the king's presence makes a lie of the words and gestures of honor that he performs when in the king's presence; it renders those words and gestures insincere, inauthentic, deviant. That, so I suggest, is what the prophets had in mind.

In closing this section of my discussion, let me note that a *deviant*

83

performance of the liturgy is not to be identified with a *defective* performance of the liturgy. One's performance of the liturgy will always be defective in one way or another. Hence it is that, in many liturgies, the concluding words of Psalm 19 occur somewhere in the liturgy:

> Let the words of my mouth and the meditations of my heart
>> be acceptable in your sight,
>> O LORD, my rock and my redeemer.

A defect commonly cited by Protestants is inattentiveness: "going through the motions." Inattentiveness is indeed a defect in one's participation in the liturgy; but it need not make one's participation deviant. In the expectation that God will listen, we pray God to forgive us not only for defects in our daily lives but also for defects in our worship, including the defect of inattentiveness.

Why Does God Listen?

There remains the most important question of all: Why does God invite us to address God, and when we do, why does God stoop down to listen to what we say? I have tried to evoke a sense of how astonishing it is that God listens to us. The more astonishing we find it that God listens to us, the more pressing becomes the question, *Why?* Why does God invite us to address God? And when we do, why does God stoop down to listen to what we say?

The answer to this question differs somewhat depending on the particular content of our address. When we praise God, we acknowledge God's unsurpassable glory; when we thank God, we acknowledge God's unsurpassable love for us. Each of these is the acknowledgment of some aspect of God's unsurpassable greatness. Having praised or thanked God, we then ask God to accept our acknowledgment of God's unsurpassable greatness in spite of the inadequacy of that acknowledgment.

The question then is this: Why would God invite us to praise and thank God for God's unsurpassable greatness, and when we do, why would God listen to what we say? A Nietzschean would see this is a prime indication of the narcissism of the Christian God. But that's to look at things from the wrong end. Though God does delight in genuine praise and thanksgiving, it's not because God revels in listening to God's greatness being acknowledged that God invites us to praise and thank God. It's because we, who have come to know God, want to acknowledge God's greatness that God invites us to feel free to do so in spite of the extreme ontological disparity between God and us, and in spite of the inevitable inadequacy of what we say. It's important to us, "right and proper," crucial to our shalom.

The commoner wants to praise the king to his face, not just behind his back. But she, a mere commoner, doesn't dare address him. The king, seeing her hesitation, invites her to do so. She does, and concludes by saying that she hopes the king will accept her inadequate words. The king listens carefully to what she says.

There is an additional point to be made here. In several Psalms the Psalmist enjoins God's non-human creatures to praise God. Psalm 148 is a good example:

> Praise [God], sun and moon;
>   praise him, all you shining stars!
> Praise him, you highest heavens,
>   and you waters above the heavens!
> Let them praise the name of the LORD,
>   for he commanded and they were created.
> He established them forever and ever;
>   he fixed their bounds.

Their presence is praise ?

The Psalmist knows that God's non-human creatures cannot literally praise God on their own. So the Psalmist praises God on their behalf. That's what he is doing when he enjoins them to praise God. He is giving voice to their praise.

Let's turn from the praise and thanksgiving that we address to God to our confession of sins and our intercessions. Following our confession we pray God to have mercy upon us and forgive us our sins. Thereby we acknowledge that we have offended God, and we appeal to God's forgiving love. Following our intercessions we pray that God will hear our prayer, that is, deliver those for whom we have interceded from what threatens their flourishing. Thereby we acknowledge our dependence on God, and appeal to God's saving love. "In the abundance of your steadfast love, answer me," prays the Psalmist.

> My prayer is to you, O LORD.
>   At an acceptable time, O God,
>   in the abundance of your steadfast love, answer me.

With your faithful help rescue me. . . .
Answer me, O LORD, for your steadfast love is good;
   according to your abundant mercy, turn to me. . . .
Draw near to me, redeem me. (69:13-18)

Why would God invite us to acknowledge our offence and dependence, and to appeal to God's love, and why would God then listen to what we say when we acknowledge that we have offended God and are dependent on God? A Nietzschean would see this as a prime indication of the wish of the Christian God to have us grovel. But this is again to look at things from the wrong end. God does not invite us to confess and intercede because God takes pleasure in listening to our acknowledgment that we have offended God and takes pleasure in listening to our acknowledgment of our dependence. God invites us to feel free to confess and intercede because we, who have come to know how we stand with God, very much want to confess and intercede — how could we not want to do so? It is "right and proper," crucial to our shalom. The king invites the commoner to feel free to do what she very much wants to do, namely, ask him for mercy and deliverance. When she does, he listens to what she says.

CHAPTER SIX

What Are We Saying
When We Say That God Listens?

Professional theologians among my readers, and those aspiring to become professional theologians, may by now be feeling uncomfortable. When I presented my project of identifying and articulating the understanding of God implicit in the Christian liturgy, you were open to seeing where this might go. You have now seen a bit of where it goes and it seems to you thin broth. You are familiar with theology that has been thickened by centuries of controversy over the Trinity, over the Incarnation, over justification, over election, over double predestination, over divine sovereignty, over divine foreknowledge, and so forth. What you have gotten in this book is thin broth by comparison. Nothing complicated. Is this what liturgical theology comes to?

Not only is it thin; it's strange in a way that's not easy to identify. It is certainly not deistic theology: no deist believes that God listens and speaks to us. Nor is it your usual generic theism. Nothing here about the familiar trio of "omni's": omnipotence, omniscience, omni-goodness. And nothing about simplicity, immutability, impassibility, eternity, and the like. But also, be it noted, nothing about God as triune or about God incarnate. Instead, God as listener and God as speaker. That's strange.

Something else may be causing discomfort as well. Isn't it patently anthropomorphic to speak of God as listening and speaking to us? Are we not making God in our own image when we speak this way? This is how children talk about God. If this is the understanding of God implicit in the liturgy, then we who are adults will either have to stop participating or contest the conclusion that the understanding of God implicit in the liturgy is that God listens and speaks. We will have to engage in a Maimonides-style analysis of the liturgy.

87

In this chapter I propose addressing the worry that we are making God in our own image when we speak of God as listening and speaking. Those who have felt uncomfortable with my discussion up to this point because of its idiosyncratic character will now find their discomfort level substantially lowered. Instead of probing the liturgy so as to make explicit what is implicit, we will be engaging the ever-so-traditional topic of the status of predications concerning God. Indeed, the discussion will feel so different from what preceded that readers may find themselves wondering whether we have left liturgical theology behind.

We will not have left it behind. I suggested that liturgical theology can be thought of as having three stages. Starting from the liturgy as a whole or from some part thereof, the liturgical theologian first tries to understand what is going on in the liturgy as a whole or in that part thereof. He then tries, second, to make explicit the understanding of God implicit therein. That done, he goes on, third, to articulate that understanding — to develop it theologically and defend it against objections. And if, along the way, he comes to the conclusion that the understanding of God implicit in some part of the liturgy is defective, he will offer a critique of that aspect of the liturgy; that critique will then also be a component of his liturgical theology.

Within which of the three stages of liturgical theology does our topic in this chapter fall, the topic, namely, of whether it is unacceptably anthropomorphic to think and speak of God as listening and speaking?

The topic can be treated in a number of different ways; depending on how it is treated, it will fall either in the first or in the third of the three stages of liturgical theology. As I will be treating it, it falls within the first stage. I have claimed that, in much of the liturgy, we are addressing God and doing so on the assumption that God listens and in the hope or expectation that God will respond favorably. I will be defending this analysis of the liturgy against an objection that comes to us from Maimonides and a good many other philosophers and theologians.

Maimonides on Why God Cannot Listen

In his *Guide of the Perplexed,* Maimonides says the following:

> Since . . . all these acts are only performed by means of bodily organs, all these organs are figuratively ascribed to [God]: those by means of

which local motion takes place — I mean the feet and their soles; those by means of which hearing, seeing, and smelling come about — that is, the ear, the eye, and the nose; those by means of which speech and the matter of speech are produced — that is, the mouth, the tongue, and the voice. . . . To sum up all this: God, may He be exalted above every deficiency, has had bodily organs ascribed to Him in order that His acts should be indicated by this means. And those particular acts are figuratively ascribed to Him in order to indicate a certain perfection, which is not identical with the particular act mentioned. . . . Action and speech are ascribed to God so that an overflow proceeding from Him should thereby be indicated; . . . organs of speech [are] mentioned with a view to indicating the overflow of the intellect toward the prophets.[1]

Taking for granted that speaking is a bodily act, Maimonides argues that, since God has no mouth, tongue, or vocal chords, God cannot literally speak. His positive proposal is that we should understand ourselves as using language figuratively when we attribute speech to God. Since our use of language is figurative, we are not engaged in anthropomorphizing.

In the passage quoted, Maimonides does not say that God cannot literally listen. There can be no doubt, however, that that was his view. Taking for granted that listening is a bodily act, he would argue that, since God has no ears or eyes, God cannot listen. And so just as we should understand ourselves as using language figuratively when we attribute speech to God, so also we should understand ourselves as using language figuratively when we attribute listening to God.

Whatever is to be said about Maimonides' positive proposal, speech-act theory makes clear that his argument for the claim that God cannot literally speak or listen is unsound. Our address to God consists of the illocutionary acts that we perform with the aim or purpose that God attend to them, grasp them, and respond favorably. We perform these illocutionary acts by performing certain locutionary acts. But it's not our utterance of a sentence with a certain meaning in mind that we address to God; it's the illocutionary act of praising God, of thanking God, of interceding with God, and so forth, that we address to God. These are not bodily actions. We perform them *by* doing something with our bodies; but they are not themselves bodily actions. They are imperceptible particulars.

1. *Guide of the Perplexed,* trans. Shlomo Pines (Chicago: University of Chicago Press, 1963), 1.46 [pp. 99-100].

Listening to what was said to one — attending to and grasping the illocutionary act performed — is likewise not a bodily action. You and I attend to and grasp the speech acts of our fellows by employing our eyes or ears; we hear the uttered sentence or see the written sentence. But our attention to, and grasping of, the illocutionary act itself is not something that we do with our eyes or ears, since that act is imperceptible. The fact that God has no eyes or ears is not a reason for holding that God cannot listen.

When the Psalmist says, "incline your ear to me,/hear my words" (17:6), we are to understand the words "incline your ear" and the word "hear" as being used figuratively; Maimonides is right about that. Literally speaking, God has no ear to incline so as to hear words. But if we are thinking along the lines of speech-act theory, we will understand the Psalmist, with this figurative use of language, as asking God to attend to the illocutionary act that he performed and to respond positively. And that illocutionary act was not something that could be seen or heard; it was imperceptible.

Of course, if it were impossible for God to attend to and grasp an illocutionary act without hearing or seeing the locutionary act whose performance *counts as* the performance of that illocutionary act, then God's lack of ears and eyes would imply that God cannot listen. But why hold that that's impossible? Recall, yet again, what it is to listen to what someone said to one. It is to attend to and grasp the illocutionary act that was performed. To attribute listening to God is thus to say of God that God attends to and understands imperceptible particulars of a certain sort, namely, illocutionary acts. If God can know the innermost secrets of our hearts, why would God be incapable of attending to and understanding the illocutionary acts that we perform?

Fair enough, you say. But to point out that listening is a species of gaining cognizance of an imperceptible particular is patently inadequate as a response to our worries about anthropomorphizing. Are we not anthropomorphizing when we attribute to God knowledge of any sort of what transpires in the world? To avoid making God in our image, don't we have to understand ourselves as speaking figuratively not only when we attribute listening to God but also when we attribute knowledge to God of any sort of spatio-temporal particular whatsoever?

Answering these questions requires that we enter the much-vexed topic of the status of predications concerning God. So that's what I will do in the remainder of this chapter.

Some Distinctions

Though the terminology used in discussing these issues is standard, different writers attach different meanings to the terms, resulting in a great deal of confusion and talking past one another; accordingly, we have to begin with some comments about terminology.

In a number of papers that he published in the 1980s, William Alston, after noting that "the impossibility of literal talk about God has become almost an article of faith for theology in this century," argued, to the contrary, that it is possible to affirm something true of God by speaking literally.[2] In the course of his argument Alston made some very helpful, clarifying remarks about the terminology standardly used when discussing these issues. A good deal of what I have to say on this matter I learned from Alston.

First, let us distinguish among various ways of using a term: we can use a term *literally,* we can use a term *figuratively,* in particular, *metaphorically,* and we can use a term with what I shall call *analogical extension.* The concept of literal and figurative use of terms is familiar; not so the concept of using a term with analogical extension. So let me explain it.

Analogical Extension

Suppose that, referring to my dog, I assertively utter the sentence, "he's a gem." I would then be using the term "gem" figuratively, more specifically, metaphorically, and I would be saying something true about my dog. Were I speaking literally, I would be saying something patently false. It has often been observed about good metaphors that a good metaphor leaves it somewhat open-ended as to what is said about the thing in question, whereas a so-called dead metaphor has almost no open-endedness about it. When I predicate "is a gem" of my dog, my metaphor is dead, or nearly so.

---

2. The essays are "Irreducible Metaphors in Theology," "Can We Speak Literally of God?" and "Functionalism and Theological Language." These essays can be found in the collection of Alston's essays titled *Divine Nature and Human Language: Essays in Philosophical Theology* (Ithaca: Cornell University Press, 1989). The quotation comes from "Irreducible Metaphors in Theology," in the aforementioned volume, p. 17. The same point about twentieth-century theology is made in a more recent book by Roger M. White, *Talking about God: The Concept of Analogy and the Problem of Religious Language* (Farnham, Surrey: Ashgate, 2010), pp. 183ff.

One additional point here: I hold that when one uses a term figuratively, one uses it with its ordinary meaning (or with one of its ordinary meanings). The difference between literal and figurative use lies not in using the term with two different meanings but in saying two quite different things, that is, performing two quite different illocutionary acts, while nonetheless using the term with the same meaning.

Now suppose that I assertively utter, again referring to my dog, "He knows his master." Suppose further that, when pressed on the matter, I admit that since we know nothing about the interior life of dogs, or whether they even have an interior life, I don't know whether it's literally true of my dog that he knows his master, or whether what's literally true of him is, rather, that he does something a good deal like that. So what I am doing, when I predicate the term "knows" of my dog, is saying that he literally either knows or does something a good deal like that. That's an example of what I mean by "using a term with analogical extension."

We use a predicate "is f" with analogical extension when we use it to say of something that it possesses the property of either *being f* or something a good deal like that. The reason I am using the predicate "is a gem" figuratively, and not with analogical extension, when I predicate it of my dog, is that I am most definitely not saying that my dog is a gem or a good deal like a gem. So too, the reason that the term "blue" is being used metaphorically, and not with analogical extension, when we speak of a blue note is that we are most definitely not saying that this sound is either blue or a good deal like the color blue. Naturally there will be borderline cases in which it's not clear whether a term is being used figuratively or with analogical extension.

In the Weekend Arts section of the *New York Times* for October 26, 2012, the music critic Zachary Woolfe recounts a conversation he had with the pianist Andras Schiff about J. S. Bach's *Well-Tempered Clavier*. Schiff is reported as describing the key of C major as snow-white, the key of B minor as deathly pitch-black, D sharp minor as pale blue, C sharp and C sharp minor as both yellow, with the latter more intense than the former. These are metaphorical uses of color terms, not analogical extensions.

Univocal, Equivocal, and Analogical

Let us move on to a new point of terminology. It is with respect to the single use of a term that one asks whether it is being used literally, figuratively, or by analogical extension. By contrast, the terms "univocal," "equivocal," and "analogical" are for making comparisons between two or more uses of a term.

If, in predicating a term of A and a term of B, we say the same thing of A and of B, our predications are univocal with respect to each other. If we say something different, our predications are equivocal with respect to each other.[3] Analogical predication is a special case of equivocal predication. Suppose that, in a case of equivocal predication, I predicate the same term of A and of B but use the term literally in one case and with analogical extension in the other case. Then my two predications are analogical with respect to each other.

Two predications of the same term can obviously be univocal with respect to each other. But the same term can also be used to make predications that are equivocal with respect to each other. For example, if the term has two established meanings and I use it literally in one of those meanings in predicating it of A and also literally, but in the other of those two meanings, in predicating it of B, then my predications are equivocal with respect to each other. Or if I use the term literally in one case and either figuratively or with analogical extension in the other case, then again my predications are equivocal with respect to each other. Another possibility for using the same term to make predications that are equivocal with respect to each other would be to use the term figuratively in both cases, with the context making clear that one is saying different things in the two cases. And even more combinations than these are possible.

Obviously different terms can be used to make predications that are equivocal with respect to each other. But they can also be used to make predications that are univocal with respect to each other. That would be the case if they are synonymous and we used them in both instances literally. It is also possible, at least with dead metaphors, to use one term literally and another metaphorically and for one's predications to be univocal with respect to each other.

The possibilities begin to seem dizzying. Let the reader be assured, however, that I have introduced these distinctions neither for their own sake nor to induce a sense of vertigo, but to bring some necessary clarity

3. Terence Cuneo has observed in correspondence that a consequence of this definition is that if I predicate F of A and not-F of B, then my predications are equivocal with respect to each other; he thinks that a satisfactory definition would avoid this consequence. I disagree. It is indeed not something that would normally be offered as an example of equivocation; but it is a case of not saying the same thing of A that I said of B.

into our discussion about predications concerning God. The main points to keep in mind are the following. It is with respect to a single use of some term that one asks whether the term is being used literally, figuratively, or with analogical extension. It is with respect to two or more predications that one asks whether the predications are univocal or equivocal with respect to each other; and if equivocal, whether or not they are analogical with respect to each other.

It's easy to confuse the idea of using a term with *analogical extension* with the idea of *analogical predications* — that is, with the idea of two *predications* being *analogical* with respect to each other. So let me highlight the difference. The concept of analogical extension pertains to the single use of some term; one can ask, concerning the single use of a term, whether or not it was used with analogical extension. It is only with respect to two or more predications that one can ask whether or not the predications are analogical with respect to each other.

Whether it is possible to say something true about God by speaking literally, or only by speaking figuratively or by analogical extension, is one question. It's a different question whether a predication of God that is true of God, and a predication of human beings that is true of human beings, can ever be univocal with respect to each other, or whether two such predications are always equivocal with respect to each other; and if they are always equivocal with respect to each other, whether in some cases they are analogical with respect to each other.

Aquinas on Predicating Terms Literally of God

Easily the most influential discussion of predications concerning God is that by Aquinas, so much so that one cannot address our topic with anything near adequacy without considering what Aquinas had to say on the matter. So let me now turn to that.[4]

We all know that Aquinas held a doctrine of analogy. It was his view that if I predicate something true of God and also predicate something true of some creature, my two predications are never univocal with respect to each other; they are always equivocal with respect to each other.

---

4. In what follows I will be borrowing from, and adapting, what I said in my essay "Alston on Aquinas on Theological Predication," in *Inquiring about God: Selected Essays,* Volume 1, ed. Terence Cuneo (Cambridge: Cambridge University Press, 2010), pp. 112-32.

Their equivocity may or may not be of such a sort as to be analogical with respect to each other.

Almost all commentators attribute to Aquinas the view that no term applies literally both to creatures and to God. Almost all of them also attribute to Aquinas the view that no term applies literally to God — that terms apply literally only to creatures. I regard it as decisively clear that Aquinas did not hold these positions. He held that some of our terms apply literally both to God and to creatures. Though predications concerning God and predications concerning creatures are at best analogical with respect to each other, never univocal, nonetheless some of our predicates apply literally both to God and to creatures. Let's see how he was thinking.

The question Aquinas poses in Part One, Question 13, Article 3 of his *Summa Theologiae* is "whether any term *(nomen)* can be said *(dicatur)* literally *(proprie)* of God?"[5] Employing the distinction between saying a term literally of some thing and saying it metaphorically of the thing, Aquinas answers that "not all terms are said metaphorically of God; but some are said literally" *(sed contra)*. These are those terms that signify "the perfections that flow from [God] and are to be found in creatures, yet which exist in [God] in an eminent way" *(resp.)*. Aquinas cites the terms "being," "good," and "living" as examples; these terms, he says, "can be said literally of God" *(ad 1)*. He assumes that they can also be said literally of creatures.

There is no reason in the text to suppose that Aquinas was not using *proprie* strictly and in its literal sense. And given that it is *metaphorice* that he contrasts with *proprie,* our term "literal" is surely the correct translation. In short, it was clearly Aquinas's view that, when using terms literally, we can affirm of God what is true of God by predicating of God such perfection terms as "exists," "good," and "living."

In the same *respondeo* *(ST* I.13.3) Aquinas amplifies and clarifies his thought by means of the distinction between that which is signified by a term, its *res significata,* and the term's mode of signification, its *modus significandi.* It is only "so far as that which is signified is concerned" that some terms "are applied literally *(proprie)* to God." Indeed, some terms are applied "more properly [to God] than to creatures, and are said primarily *(per prius)* of God." With respect to mode of signification, however, there

5. Neither the Dominican nor the Blackfriars translation of the *Summa Theologiae* is entirely satisfactory for my purposes, since both misinterpret Aquinas on the very points that I will be discussing. In general, however, I will be following the Dominican translation, on the ground that it is more literal, and revising where I deem it necessary.

are no terms that can be "literally *(proprie)* said of God; for they [all] have a mode of signification that is relevant to creatures" *(resp.)*.

Aquinas assumes that his readers are familiar with the distinction between the *res significata* of a term and its *modus significandi;* he does not explain the distinction. What is meant by the *res significata* of a predicate term is clear — or given that many predicate terms have a number of distinct meanings, what's clear is what is meant by the *res significata* of a-predicate-term-with-a-certain-meaning. It's the property "signified" or designated by the term with that meaning — that is, the property that one would attribute to something if, speaking literally, one predicated the predicate with that meaning. When it is perfection terms that we are using, the *res significata* is the perfection that the term designates (signifies): goodness, life, existence, and so forth.

What Aquinas had in mind by the *modus significandi* of a term is less clear, though still clear enough for our purposes here. We get the essential information in his remark that "our intellect apprehends these perfections in the mode that they are present in creatures." I think we will not go astray if we think of the mode of signification of a predicate term as included in what we would nowadays call its connotations.

Take any case of apprehending some property, any case of having the property in mind. Aquinas distinguishes between, on the one hand, the property apprehended, and, on the other hand, one's way of apprehending it. One's way of apprehending it is shaped by one's familiarity with the way in which that property is present in creatures. Thus when I am thinking of *power,* one can distinguish between what I am apprehending, namely, power, and my way of apprehending it, this latter being shaped by the powerful things with which I am familiar. Of course, not only do I apprehend the property, power; you do so as well, along with most other human beings out of infancy. Hence we can speak not just of my way of apprehending power and of your way of apprehending power, but of *our* way of apprehending power.

Aquinas's thought is that the distinction between the property we apprehend, and our way of apprehending it, is carried over into, or preserved within, the corresponding predicate term. Aspects of our way of apprehending some perfection in our creaturely experience become ingredients in the mode of signification of a term that signifies that perfection — ingredients in its connotation. A predicate term will not only signify a certain property; it will also express — "express" is probably the best word here — our way of apprehending those instantiations of that property familiar to us from our experience. And whatever else may be true of such experiences of ours, they will all have been experiences of creatures.

Aquinas employs his distinction between the *res significata* of a term and its *modus significandi* to explain why it is that some terms can be predicated literally of God and some only metaphorically. "Those terms that are said literally of God do not include bodily conditions in that which is signified but only in their mode of signification, whereas those that are said *(dicuntur)* metaphorically of God include bodily conditions in the very thing signified" (*ST* I.13.3. *ad* 3). Speaking more elaborately, he says this:

> There are some names which signify these perfections flowing from God to creatures in such a way that the imperfect way in which creatures receive the divine perfection is part of the very signification of the name itself, as *stone* signifies a material being; and names of this kind can be applied *(attribui)* to God only in a metaphorical sense. Other names, however, signify these perfections absolutely, without any such mode of participation being part of their signification, as the words *being, good, living,* and the like, and such names can be literally said *(dicuntur)* of God. (*ST* I.13.5)

Aquinas on Predications That Are Analogous with Respect to Each Other

Two articles later, in the same question on "The Names of God," Aquinas poses a new question, namely, "whether terms are said univocally or equivocally of God and creatures" (*ST* I.13.5). Aquinas does not assume that this question has already been answered in what he has said about the literality of speech about God; our discussion about terminology shows that he is right about that. The point is so often overlooked as to be worth repeating one more time. When considering whether a term has been used literally or figuratively, one takes a single instance of its use and poses one's question concerning that particular use. It makes no sense to ask, concerning a single use, whether it is used univocally or equivocally. It is only with reference to two or more predications of some term that one can raise the question whether the predications are univocal or equivocal with respect to each other, and if equivocal, whether they are analogical with respect to each other. Predications are never just analogical, *period.* They are only ever analogical *with respect to each other.*

To the question, whether terms are said univocally or equivocally of God and of creatures, Aquinas's answer is that "it is impossible to predicate *(praedicare)* anything univocally of God and creatures. That which is predicated *(praedicatur)* of several things according to the same term, but not according to the same *ratio,* is predicated of them equivocally. But no term applies *(convenit)* to God with that *ratio* according to which it is said *(dicitur)* of a creature." The two predications will always be equivocal with respect to each other. Using the term "is wise" as his example, Aquinas then says, "For wisdom in creatures is a quality, though not in God" *(ST* I.13.5).

A Puzzle, and Its Solution

A puzzle now confronts us. Aquinas has insisted that perfection terms are literally true not just of us but of God, his reason being that the *res significata* of those perfection terms is just those perfections themselves, not any particular way of instantiating the perfections. Our creaturely ways of instantiating the perfections do not enter into the *res significata* of the terms; they enter into their connotations or mode of signification, but not into what is signified. Yet as between God and creatures, neither perfection terms nor any others are ever predicated univocally. How can this be? How can the same term in the same sense apply literally both to God and to us, and yet our predications not be univocal with respect to each other?

Begin with Aquinas's reason for holding that affirmative predications as between God and human beings are never univocal with respect to each other. Aquinas leaves us in no doubt as to why he holds this position. It's because God is ontologically simple, a position he has argued for earlier *(ST* I.3), whereas no creature is ontologically simple. In God there is no distinction between God and God's essence, between God and God's attributes, between one of God's attributes and another of God's attributes. It is this that Aquinas was alluding to when he said that the reason "is wise" cannot be predicated univocally of God and of creatures is that "wisdom in creatures is a quality, though not in God" *(ST* I.13.5). What he means by "a quality" is an attribute distinct from the substance of which it is the attribute.

Suppose, now, that you and I hold Aquinas's ontology: creatures are ontologically complex whereas God is ontologically simple; nonetheless, we participate in the same perfections. What would we then say on the topic of the univocity or equivocity of predications concerning God and creatures?

I submit that we would say the following. Given our conviction that God and we participate in the same perfections, we would say that in assertively uttering "God is alive," "God is good," "God is powerful," and the like, the adjectives "alive," "good," and "powerful" designate or signify the same perfections that they do when, referring to some human being, we assertively utter "he is alive," "he is good," or "he is powerful." In assertively uttering about God, "God is alive," and assertively uttering about Joe, "Joe is alive," we are predicating the same "form" of these two very different beings. And in both cases we are using the adjective "alive" literally.

We would not drop the matter there, however. Given our other conviction, that God "participates" in perfections as a simple being whereas we participate in them as complex beings, we would say that in predicating "is alive" of God and of Joe, we are claiming a different relationship to hold in the two cases between the entity and its perfection. Though the adjective "alive" has the same sense in both cases, the copula "is" does not. In predicating "is alive" of both God and Joe, our predications are univocal with respect to the adjective but equivocal with respect to the copula.

I said that this is what we would say if we embraced Aquinas's ontology. And this is what Aquinas does say. Let me quote again the passage quoted just above in which Aquinas declares that all predications as between God and creatures are equivocal. "That which is predicated of several things according to the same term, but not according to the same *ratio,* is predicated of them equivocally. But no term applies *(convenit)* to God with that *ratio* according to which it is said *(dicitur)* of a creature." Even if the term is the same, it is not *predicated* according to the same *ratio,* that is, with the same import; the predicating does not have the same import. The term does not *apply* to God according to the same *ratio,* that is, with the same import; our *application* of the term does not have the same import. To say it again: our predication of the same perfection term to God and to creatures is univocal with respect to the adjective but equivocal with respect to the copula.

It is not, however, *merely* equivocal with respect to the copula. The import *(ratio)* of the copula in the two cases is not completely different and unconnected; the copula is not being used *purely* equivocally. Its import *(ratio)* when predicating something of God is an *analogical extension of* its import *(ratio)* when predicating something of creatures. In both cases one is claiming some mode of "participation" in the perfection by the entity referred to. God's relation to the perfection designated by the adjective is something like our relation to the perfection. When we predicate "is alive" of God, we are using the term "alive" literally whereas we are using the copula with *analogical extension.*

In short, Aquinas's doctrine of analogy pertains to the act of predicating, not to what is predicated. More precisely, it pertains to the copula, not to the adjective. When we predicate "is wise" both of God and of some human being, our predications are univocal with respect to the adjective but analogical with respect to the copula. And by now it should go without saying that to say of our two predications that they are analogical with respect to the copula is fully compatible with saying of the adjective that it is being used literally in both cases.

I can imagine someone replying that the interpretation of Aquinas that I have just now offered is a radical over-interpretation of his extremely brief comments about the *ratio* of predications in the *sed contra* of *ST* I.13.5. My response is that perhaps it would be over-interpretation if that passage were the full extent of what Aquinas had to say on the matter. But it's not. That analogy pertains to the copula and not to the adjective seems to me the clear teaching of the *respondeo* of I.13.5. Here is what Aquinas says:

> Univocal predication is impossible between God and creatures. The reason for this is that every effect which is not an adequate result of the power of the efficient cause receives the similitude of the agent not in its full degree, but in a measure that falls short, so that what is divided and multiplied in the effects resides in the agent simply, and in the same manner; as for example the sun by the exercise of its own power produces manifold and various forms in all inferior things. In the same way, . . . all perfections existing in creatures divided and multiplied, pre-exist in God unitedly. Thus when some term pertaining to a perfection is said of a creature, it signifies that particular perfection in distinction from others. For example, when the term "wise" is said of a human being, we signify a perfection distinct from the essence of the person, from his powers, his existence, and from all the other things about him. But when we say this term of God, we do not intend to signify something distinct from his essence, or power, or existence. . . . Hence it is clear that this term "wise" is not said of God and of a human being according to the same *ratio*. The same point holds for other terms. Accordingly, no term is predicated univocally of God and

creatures. But also not purely *(pure)* equivocally, as some have said. . . . Therefore it must be said that terms are said of God and of creatures according to analogy, that is, proportion.

This is Aquinas's argument for holding that our predication of perfection terms is equivocal as between God and human beings. His argument for holding that it is nonetheless not *purely* equivocal but instead analogical goes as follows:

> Whatever is said of God and creatures is said according to the relation of a creature to God as its principle and cause, wherein all perfections of things pre-exist excellently. Now this mode of community of idea is a mean between pure equivocation and simple univocation. For in analogies the idea is not, as it is in univocals, one and the same, yet it is not totally diverse as in equivocals; but a term which is thus used in a multiple sense signifies various proportions to some one thing. (*ST* I.13.5, *resp.*)

We have been looking at Aquinas's discussion of predications concerning God in his *Summa Theologiae*. Aquinas also treated the topic in his earlier *Summa Contra Gentiles*. There it is, if anything, even more clear that it is in the copula and not in the adjective that Aquinas located the analogy required by his doctrine of divine simplicity. Here is what he says:

> An effect that does not receive a form specifically the same as that through which the agent acts cannot receive according to a univocal predication the name arising from that form. . . . Now, the forms of the things God has made do not measure up to a specific likeness of the divine power: for the things that God has made receive in a divided and particular way that which in Him is found in a simple and universal way. It is evident, then, that nothing can be said univocally of God and other things. (*SCG* I.32.2)

Notice that the way forms in things are said not to "measure up to" forms in God is just that God receives forms in a simple way and we receive forms in a divided way. It is for that reason that nothing can be said univocally of God and of us. The saying-of, the predicating-of, is what is not univocal as between predications of God and of us; the adjectives predicated may designate the same perfection in both cases.

Aquinas continues as follows:

> If, furthermore, an effect should measure up to the species of its cause, it will not receive the univocal predication of the name unless it receives the same form according to the same mode of being. For the form of the house that is in the art of the maker is not univocally the same being in the two locations. Now, even though the rest of things were to receive a form that is absolutely the same as it is in God, yet they do not receive it according to the same mode of being. For as is clear from what we have said, there is nothing in God that is not the divine being itself which is not the case with other things. Nothing, therefore, can be predicated of God and other things univocally. (*SCG* I.32.3)

The same perfection terms apply literally both to God and to creatures with respect to their *res significata*. It is the *act of predicating* that is not univocal — or more precisely, the force *(ratio)* of the copula.

English Translations Conceal Aquinas's Thought

That Aquinas was thinking along these lines is concealed from us by our standard English translations. Let me offer two examples of the point. Consider, once again, the two sentences that I quoted from the *sed contra* of *ST* I.13.5:

> That which is predicated of several things according to the same term, but not according to the same *ratio*, is predicated of them equivocally. But no term applies *(convenit)* to God with that *ratio* according to which it is said *(dicitur)* of a creature.

The Blackfriars translation, by Herbert McCabe, O.P., renders the second sentence as follows: "but no word when used of God means the same as when it is used of a creature." I have no idea how McCabe harmonizes his translation of this passage with the claim Aquinas made, just two articles earlier, that perfection terms apply literally to God and to us. But be that as it may. This is interpretation, not translation. Aquinas does not say what McCabe has him saying, namely, that no term *means the same* when used of God as when used of a creature. The Latin is this: "sed nullum nomen convenit Deo secundum illam rationem, secundum quam dicitur de creature." Literally: "But no name applies to God according to the same *ratio* according to which it is said of a creature." What Aquinas says is that no term *is said of* God and of creatures according to the same *ratio;* he does not say that the term never means the same in the two cases.

Consider, further, the passage from the *respondeo* of *ST* I.13.5 that I translated this way: "Hence it is clear that this term 'wise' is not said of *(dicitur)* God and of a human being according to the same *ratio.* The same point holds for other terms." The Blackfriars translation renders the passage as follows: "Hence it is clear that the word 'wise' is not used in the same sense of God and man, and the same is true of all other words." But Aquinas does not say that the term "wise" is not used in the same sense. He says that the term is not *said of (dicitur)* God and of creatures according to the same *ratio.*

Speaking for Ourselves on the Matter

The reader may have noticed that whereas I distinguished between using a term literally, using a term figuratively, and using a term with analogical extension, Aquinas distinguished only between the literal and the metaphorical uses of terms. (I assume that when he spoke of metaphorical uses, it was figurative uses in general that he had in mind.) I hold that we need the idea of using a term with metaphorical extension to identify, for example, how the term "knows" is being used when I say of my dog that it knows its master. Quite clearly it's not a figurative use of the term. It's not like saying of my dog that he is a gem, nor is it like describing the key of D sharp minor as pale blue. But given that we know nothing about the inner life of a dog, I do not know, speaking literally, whether my dog knows its master, whereas I do know, speaking literally, that it has four legs. So I suggested that when I predicate "knows his master," I am saying that either he knows his master or does something a good deal like that. I am employing the term with analogical extension.

As we saw, what motivated Aquinas to introduce the idea of predications that are analogous with respect to the copula was his doctrine of divine simplicity. The doctrine of divine simplicity has had a profound influence on theology. In Aquinas's case, it was the first conclusion he drew from his argument that reality is such that there must be something that is the unconditioned condition of all that is not identical with itself. A simple being is one within which there is no distinction of any sort whatsoever. If, say, God's essence were distinct from God himself, then God would be conditioned by something distinct from God, namely, God's essence.

Given the degree to which the doctrine of divine simplicity has shaped Christian theology, a theologian or philosopher who is a member of the Christian tradition, such as myself, does not discard the doctrine lightly. Nonetheless, I think it should be discarded.

Some have argued that the doctrine is ultimately incoherent.[6] Though it is indeed true that it cannot be given coherent articulation within certain ontological frameworks, I have argued elsewhere that it can be given coherent articulation within an Aristotelian framework — which, of course, was the framework that Aquinas was using.[7] Among my reasons for thinking the doctrine should nonetheless be discarded are the following two. I do not find the argument compelling, that reality is such that there has to be something that is the unconditioned condition of all that is not identical with itself. And, more important, the doctrine seems to me ultimately incompatible with the doctrine of God as triune. To say that God is triune is perforce to say that there is some sort of distinction within God, a distinction of *persons,* to use the traditional concept.[8]

What my rejection of divine simplicity implies is that I have no need for Aquinas's idea of predications concerning God and creatures that are equivocal with respect to the copula but univocal with respect to the predicate. On my view, the copula is used with the same import when speaking of God and of creatures.

God is vastly beyond our comprehension. We have no idea, none at all, as to how God creates. We have no idea, none at all, as to how God sustains the universe. Quite clearly creation does require something rather like knowledge, however; hence it is that over and over the Psalmist celebrated the wisdom of God. My suggestion is that when we apply the term "knows" to God, we are using the term with analogical extension. When we say of God that God is the rock of our salvation, we are using the term "rock" metaphorically, as a figure of speech. Saying of God that God knows is not like that. "Knows" is not being employed metaphorically, as a figure

---

6. See Alvin Plantinga, *Does God Have a Nature?* (Milwaukee: Marquette University Press, 1980).

7. See my essay "Divine Simplicity" in *Inquiring about God,* pp. 91-111.

8. I am aware of the fact that Aquinas tried to develop a doctrine of the Trinity that is compatible with divine simplicity. It seems to me that his attempt is not successful; here is obviously not the place to argue the point.

of speech. We are saying, so I suggest, that God either knows or does something a good deal like knowing. It follows that our predications of "knows" of creatures and of God are analogical with respect to each other. "Knows" is literally true of us and true by analogical extension of God.

As a warrant for interpreting the term "knows" when applied to God as used neither literally nor figuratively but with analogical extension, I said that the creation and preservation of the universe requires, if not knowledge, then something a good deal like knowledge. There is another consideration that is relevant as well.

The writer of Genesis declares that we have been created in the image of God, in the likeness of God. Nothing of the sort is said about the other animals. As we all know, the writer gives no explanation of what is meant by saying that we are created in the image and likeness of God. The context provides a few hints, but only a few, with the result that there have been mountains of speculation on the matter. But given that no other animals are said to have been made in the image and likeness of God, one infers that it has something to do with our being persons — personic animals, animalic persons. Our capacity for knowledge is a central component in our personhood. It's hard to resist the conclusion that we image God in our capacity for knowledge.

In the order of attribution, we learn how to apply the term "knows" to human persons and then apply it by analogical extension to God. In the order of things, what we call knowledge in us is an image of something that is a good deal like that in God. Aquinas generalizes the point by saying that perfections flow from God to us.

Is It a Figure of Speech to Say of God That God Listens and Speaks?

Let us return to the question with which we began. Unless one is speaking figuratively, is it not a painfully childish anthropomorphism to say of God that God listens and speaks? Is not a Maimonides-style analysis of the liturgy required at this point?

What we saw earlier is that when one attends to and grasps what was said to one, neither the speech act that one attends to and grasps, nor the actions of attending to and grasping it, are as such bodily actions. In your and my case, we perform these actions *by way of* performing certain bodily actions; but the actions are not themselves bodily. I see no reason to doubt that God can attend to and grasp what we say to God even though God has no body. God cannot taste strawberries; one needs a tongue for that. Not so for attending to and grasping the illocutionary acts that we perform. And as to how we are using the terms "attend to" and "grasp" when we apply them to God, we are not using them figuratively but with analogical extension. To say of God that God attends to and grasps what we say to God is to say of God that God either attends to and grasps what we say to God or does something a good deal like that. We are not engaged in childish anthropomorphisms.

Everything I have said about how we should understand the claim that God listens to us applies also, with appropriate adaptations, to how we should understand the claim that God speaks to us. When we say of God that God speaks, we are using the term "speaks" with analogical extension.

Aquinas, along with many others, recognizes only two ways of using terms: literally and figuratively. I hold that between those two ways of using a term lies using a term with analogical extension. When saying that God listens and speaks, we are not impaled on the dilemma of either speaking literally and hence thinking anthropomorphically, or speaking figuratively. We are using the terms "listens" and "speaks" with analogical extension.

CHAPTER SEVEN

God as One Who Hears Favorably

In the liturgy, after addressing God in praise and thanksgiving, we add the words, "May our sacrifice of praise and thanksgiving be acceptable in your sight, O Lord." After confessing our sins and asking God for forgiveness, we add the words, "Lord have mercy, Christ have mercy." After addressing our supplications to God, we add the words, "Hear our prayer, O Lord."

Having addressed God on the assumption that God is listening, we then ask God to hear favorably our praise, our thanksgiving, our plea for forgiveness, our supplications. The question before us in this chapter is, what is the understanding of God implicit in this repeated liturgical action of asking God to hear favorably our address to God?

In asking God to hear our address favorably, we are evidently assuming that God *can* respond to our sacrifice of praise and thanksgiving by accepting it, that God *can* respond to our plea for forgiveness by offering forgiveness, and that God *can* respond to our supplications by granting what we ask. Evidently the understanding of God implicit in these liturgical actions is that God can respond to our address.

Once that is noted, however, Maimonides-style worries immediately arise in the mind of anyone versed in the tradition of philosophical theology. Can God really respond, literally speaking? Is it not incompatible with God's aseity, with God's eternity, and with God's immutability, for God to respond to what we say? Do we not need an alternative, Maimonides-style analysis of what we are doing at this point in the liturgy, an analysis that does not presuppose that, speaking literally or by analogical extension, God can respond? And as for our supplications, it would appear that we are taking for granted that God *can* respond by intervening in the causal order. But can God really intervene in the causal order, speaking literally or by analogical extension? And if God can intervene, is there any reason to suppose that God does? Much of what we intercede with God to do never happens. Do we not, at this point also, need a skeptical, Maimonides-style analysis of the liturgy?

To plunge immediately into one or another of these much-vexed questions from the tradition of philosophical theology would be to assume that we know the significance of asking God to hear our address favorably. But do we? Rather than just assuming that we know the significance of this added-on address to God, I propose that we stand back and reflect on its significance.

The Significance of Asking God to Hear Favorably

Why don't we voice our praise, our thanksgiving, our plea for forgiveness, our supplications, and let it go at that? Why do we add the plea that God hear favorably what we have said?

As I noted in a previous chapter, the church did not just come up with this addition. In appending this addition to its praise, its thanksgiving, its plea for forgiveness, and its supplications, the church has followed the lead of the Psalmist. Over and over, dozens of times in multiple variations, the Psalmist asks for God's favorable hearing: "hear my prayer," "incline your ear," "hasten to answer me," "hear my voice," "hear my words," "answer me," "give heed to my cry."

Some of the significance of the addition is obvious: God's invitation to us to address God does not carry the implication that we can now just take for granted that God will hear favorably whatever we say. God's hearing favorably what we say is an act of grace and favor on God's part. It's not something God *must* do. It's not something that our address *exacts* from God. Our prayer, that God will hear favorably our address, is our acknowledgment that it is an act of free grace on God's part to hear favorably what we say.

That much is clear. But what exactly is it that we are asking God graciously to do? Take, for example, our supplications. Are we just singling out things that we would like to happen and asking God to intervene in the causal order and bring them about, doing this on the off-chance that God will bring about at least some of what we ask? Do we pray for the healing of friends, relatives, and fellow congregants and then, if healing occurs, conclude that God heard favorably in this case whereas, if healing does not occur, conclude that, for reasons hidden from us, God did not hear favorably?

If that is what we are doing, namely, singling out various things that we would like to happen on the off-chance that God will bring about some of them if we ask God to do so, what is the appropriate stance or mood on our part? Is the appropriate stance hope? Do we pray in the *hope* that, from all the supplications addressed to God, God will select ours for favorable hearing? Or is the appropriate stance wish? Are we expressing the *wish* that God will select our request for favorable hearing? Or is the appropriate stance, sometimes at least, desperation? Do we sometimes imitate the Psalmist when he cries out in desperation, "Out of the depths I cry to you, O LORD! LORD, hear my voice! Let your ears be attentive to the voice of my supplications" (130:1-2)? Or do we, as Scripture sometimes suggests, pray with confidence? Confidence in what?

Once again, what exactly are we asking God to do when we ask God to hear favorably our address to God? How are we to understand this liturgical act?

May Your Kingdom Come

In all traditional liturgies, among the prayers that the people offer to God is the Lord's Prayer. That this is not just one among others is indicated by the fact that it is introduced by words indicating that this is the prayer our Lord spoke when he was asked by one of his disciples, "Lord, teach us to pray" (Luke 11:1). In the Episcopal liturgy the celebrant says: "And now, as our Savior Christ taught us, we are bold to say." In short, this, for the church, is the paradigmatic prayer. All other prayers in the liturgy are to be understood as variations on, or amplifications of, this prayer. If some prayer cannot be so understood, then it has no place in the liturgy. Or to speak more cautiously: then its place in the liturgy will have to be defended on some other ground than that, in praying this particular prayer, we are praying as our Lord taught us to pray.

After the opening address, "Our Father in heaven," and the first petition, that God's name be hallowed, we pray, "your kingdom come." We then ask that God's will be done on earth as it is in heaven, that God give us this day our daily bread, that God forgive us our debts as we forgive our debtors, and that God deliver us from the time of trial and from the grip of evil. We then conclude our petitions with the words, "For yours is the kingdom, the power, and the glory."

The basic question to ask concerning this paradigmatic prayer is how we are to understand the role, in the prayer as a whole, of the petition that God's kingdom come and the echo of this petition in the closing declaration that the kingdom is God's. Are we to understand this petition as just one among the others, on a level, for example, with the petition that God give us this day our daily bread?[1]

I submit that that would be a serious misinterpretation. The prayer as a whole is to be understood as framed by the petition that God's kingdom come and by the closing declaration that the kingdom is God's. The other petitions are to be understood as occurring within this frame.[2]

We offer these prayers in the conviction that the kingdom is God's. In that conviction, we pray for the coming of God's kingdom, that is, for its ever-fuller manifestation. In God's kingdom God's name will be hallowed; hence it is that we pray, "hallowed be your name." In God's kingdom God's will shall be done; that's why we pray, "your will be done, on earth as it is in heaven." In God's kingdom we will enjoy sustenance sufficient for our daily lives; hence it is that we pray, "give us this day our daily bread." In God's kingdom God will forgive us our debts and we will forgive those in debt to us; hence it is that we pray, "forgive us our debts, as we forgive our debtors." In God's kingdom we will no longer be faced with trials and will be released from the grip of evil; hence it is that we pray, "lead us not into temptation but deliver us from evil."

In short, within the frame constituted by our declaration that the kingdom is God's and by our prayer for its ever-fuller manifestation, we mention signs of the kingdom and pray for the presence of those signs: when the kingdom is fully manifested God's name will be hallowed, God's will shall be done, we will have sustenance sufficient for our daily lives, we will be forgiven even as we forgive, we will no longer be faced with trials and will be released from the grip of evil. To mention these signs of the kingdom is at the same time, of course, to allude to ways in which God's

1. Calvin, in his exposition of the Lord's Prayer in the *Institutes,* treats the petition for the coming of the kingdom as just one among the six petitions (III.xx.34-47). He further says that the second petition is a "similar and almost identical entreaty" to the first (III. xx.42; p. 905).

2. Here is how the twentieth-century Dutch Reformed theologian K. H. Miskotte puts the point, that all prayers are (or should be) kingdom prayers: "All genuine prayers for the small and large, personal or general things, about living, working, saving, and helping, are related to the *coming of the reign of God,* as the fulfillment of God's promise." Quoted in F. Gerrit Immink, *The Touch of the Sacred: The Practice, Theology, and Tradition of Christian Worship* (Grand Rapids: William B. Eerdmans Publishing Company, 2014), p. 145.

kingdom is not yet fully manifested. God's name is not universally hallowed, not everybody has sustenance sufficient for daily life, many practice vengeance rather than forgiveness, many remain in the grip of one and another form of evil: in the grip of addictions, ideological "isms," and the like.

Given that this is the paradigmatic prayer, and given that in this prayer our petitions are set in the context of declaring that the kingdom is God's and of petitioning God for the full manifestation of God's kingdom, the conclusion, surely, is that our prayers in general are not to consist of, and are not to be understood as consisting of, asking God for things in addition to the coming of God's kingdom. They are not to consist of, and are not to be understood as consisting of, asking God to intervene in the causal order so as to bring about various things that we very much want to happen in addition to the coming of God's kingdom. They are instead to be understood as the church's concrete expression of her longing for the full manifestation of God's kingdom. By "concrete expression" I mean that, rather than being content with a generalized expression of longing, we name concrete points of longing. "May Ruth be healed." "May our tyrannical regime be overthrown."

The question whose answer we have been pursuing is, what is the understanding of God implicit in the liturgical act of asking God to hear favorably our praise, our thanksgiving, our plea for forgiveness, our supplications. To answer the question we had to get clear on what exactly it is that we are asking God to do when we ask God to hear favorably our address. The answer to our question is now immediately before us: the understanding of God implicit in our liturgical act of asking God to hear favorably our address to God is that of God as actively engaged in bringing about the full manifestation of God's kingdom.

Two Understandings of God's Kingdom

And what is God's kingdom? In the Nicene Creed, recited in the enactment of many traditional liturgies, we declare of Christ that "he will come again in glory to judge the living and the dead, and his kingdom will have no end." In the prayers of the people within the Rite for Holy Communion of the Episcopal Church the people pray that, with all the saints who have died, they "may be partakers of thy heavenly kingdom" (330). In the alternative Form VI for the prayers of the people they pray, "for all who have died, that they may have a place in your eternal kingdom" (393). In Rite

Two for Holy Communion the celebrant includes, in the Great Thanksgiving, the petition that "at the last day [you will] bring us with all your saints into the joy of your eternal kingdom" (363). In that same Rite the celebrant and people thank God, after Communion, for assuring them that they are "heirs of your eternal kingdom." In Rite One for the Holy Eucharist they thank God, after Communion, that they are "heirs, through hope, of thy everlasting kingdom" (339).

There can be no doubt whatsoever that the understanding of the kingdom of God coming to expression in the Creed and in these prayers is a different understanding from that coming to expression in the Lord's Prayer. What the prayers refer to as God's "heavenly," "eternal," or "everlasting" kingdom is not the same as the kingdom whose coming is marked, among other things, by the fact that people have sufficient sustenance for their daily lives and are released from the grip of evil. By "the kingdom of God," the Creed and the prayers mean the age of consummation, the Age of the Resurrection. The word "eternal" strongly suggests that it's a kingdom that lies outside our world of space and time. The liturgy of the Episcopal Church is not at all peculiar in that this is what is meant when it speaks of God's kingdom; it is, on the contrary, typical.

Within these liturgies there is, thus, tension. When they speak of God's kingdom, it is typically to the Age of the Resurrection that they are referring; yet they include, among the prayers of the liturgy, the Lord's Prayer, where the reference is clearly to something for whose coming here and now we pray, in this place and time. Of course the kingdom for whose coming here and now we pray is not wholly disconnected from God's kingdom in the age to come: insofar as we have bread sufficient for the day, insofar as we are delivered from the grip of evil, insofar as we forgive and are forgiven, we experience a foretaste of life in that eternal kingdom. Indeed, our enactment of the liturgy is itself a foretaste of that eternal kingdom. So it's right that there should be tension on this point within the liturgy. What's not right, so I suggest, is that references in the liturgy to God's eternal kingdom should come so close to overwhelming references to the coming of God's kingdom in this present age.

The Coming of God's Kingdom

Where shall we look for an articulation or elaboration of the understanding of God's kingdom being employed in the Lord's Prayer and presupposed by the plea, scattered throughout the liturgy, "Hear our prayer, O Lord"? Not, I suggest, to the speculative ruminations concerning the kingdom of God by one or another theologian, but to whatever sources will illuminate for us what Jesus had in mind. Fortunately, we now have available to us a guide to and through those sources that is, in my judgment, without peer — though I hasten to add that this judgment comes from one who has no expertise in the field whatsoever.

The guide I have in mind is the extraordinarily comprehensive, thorough, perceptive, and balanced discussion by N. T. Wright in his 1996 publication, *Jesus and the Victory of God,* and in his 2012 popular presentation of the same material in *How God Became King.*[3] Every other discussion of the kingdom of God that I have read seems to me thin, pallid, and misleading in comparison. Wright's discussion displays thorough acquaintance with the relevant original texts and massive acquaintance with the secondary literature. And it is refreshingly clear of glib Enlightenment and post-Enlightenment skepticism. The books are lengthy: *Jesus and the Victory of God* has 662 pages of text, *How God Became King* has 276 pages. Here I can do no more than present the heart of the matter. A good deal of my presentation will consist of quotations.

Near the opening of his discussion in *How God Became King,* Wright observes that "The great creeds, when they refer to Jesus, pass directly from his virgin birth to his suffering and death. The four gospels don't. Or, to put it the other way around, Matthew, Mark, Luke, and John all seem to think it's hugely important that they tell us a great deal about what Jesus did between the time of his birth and the time of his death. In particular, they tell us about what we might call his kingdom-inaugurating work: the deeds and words that declared that God's kingdom was coming then and there, in some sense or other, on earth as in heaven. They tell a great deal about that; but the great creeds don't" (11). Wright quotes the section of the Apostles' Creed about Jesus Christ and then wryly observes, "So much detail, and yet nothing at all about what Jesus did in between being conceived and born, on the one hand, and being crucified under Pontius Pilate, on the other" (13). What is true of the creeds is true, as well, of many of the prayers in the liturgy. The Great Thanksgiving in the Episcopal *Book of Common Prayer* goes straight from the incarnation to the crucifixion.

---

3. N. T. Wright, *Jesus and the Victory of God* (Minneapolis: Fortress, 1996); *How God Became King* (New York: Harper One, 2012). I thank Edwin van Driel for referring me to these volumes. My references will be incorporated into the text.

The reason for this striking gap in the creeds is, of course, that the creeds were the outcome of intense and extended controversies in the early church over the nature of the Incarnation and the Trinity. Nothing that Jesus was reported as having done or said between his birth and his death proved particularly controversial in the early centuries of the church. Hence "no need to mention the central substance of the gospels in the creeds." Wright observes that this has had a "massive," albeit "completely unintended consequence." It is, he says, one of the major reasons "why Christians to this day find it so hard to grasp what the gospels [were] really trying to say" (12).

From Wright's discussion it becomes clear that there is another, even weightier, reason why we find it so hard to grasp what the gospels were trying to say about the kingdom-inaugurating words and works of Jesus. Wright argues compellingly in *Jesus and the Victory of God* that "the old picture of Jesus as the teacher of timeless truths, or even the announcer of the essentially timeless call for decision, will simply have to go" (172).[4] To understand what the gospels were trying to say we have to enter the thought-world of first-century Jews; what the gospels were trying to say about the kingdom-inaugurating words and works of Jesus was a variation on that thought-world. But to us, members of early twenty-first-century Western societies, that thought-world is profoundly strange. It's somewhat less strange to those of us who are Christians than it is to our secular neighbors. Yet to us too it is strange, more than strange, weird. It's hard to get into, miles away from how we are accustomed to think.

Jesus and the Kingdom of God

The gospels, says Wright, "suggest that Jesus was seen as, and saw himself as, *a* prophet, . . . a prophet like the prophets of old, coming to Israel with a word from her covenant god warning her of the imminent and fearful consequences of the direction she was travelling, urging and summoning her to a new and different way" (163), and grouping around himself a company who "would be regarded as the true people of YHWH" (196). He traveled from village to village with an entourage of twelve disciples, proclaiming the imminent coming of the kingdom of God. His proclamation took the

---

4. Unless otherwise indicated, all subsequent references in this section of my argument are to Wright's *Jesus and the Victory of God*.

form of parables, judgments of doom, and sayings, often cryptic; it took the form of actions symbolic of the coming of the kingdom, such as his entrance into Jerusalem, his cleansing of the Temple, and his last supper; and it took the form of actions that bestowed shalom and were thus indicative of the breaking in of the kingdom, such as healings, exorcisms, declarations of forgiveness, and meals with religious and social outcasts.

The impression one gets from the gospels is that the parables, the judgments of doom, the sayings, and so forth, were each delivered once; biblical critics then try to explain why the reports of what Jesus said vary somewhat from gospel to gospel. But surely this impression is mistaken. In traveling from village to village Jesus would have performed healings and exorcisms in many villages, would have had meals with outcasts in many houses, would have delivered the same sayings many times, told the same parables, issued the same judgments of doom, no doubt with slight variations. What each of the gospels gives us is, as it were, a composite picture in which the most memorable incidents are highlighted. Let me quote Wright: "Within the peasant oral culture of his day, Jesus must have left behind him, not one or two isolated traditions, but a veritable mare's nest of anecdotes, and also of sentences, aphorisms, rhythmic sayings, memorable stories with local variations, and words that were remembered because of their pithy and apposite phrasing, and because of their instantly being repeated by those who had heard them" (170).

What would a Palestinian Jew in the first half of the first century have understood an itinerant prophet to be saying when the prophet declared that the kingdom of God was about to arrive? Or to put the same question in other words: what would he or she have understood a prophet to be saying when the prophet declared that God was about to become king? There is no mystery in how they would have understood the claim that some human being was about to become king. But how would they have understood the claim that God would shortly become king, that the kingdom of God was at hand?

As Wright wryly observes, they would not have understood it as the claim "that the space-time universe [was] about to come to an end, or that a transcendent figure [was] about to come floating, cloudborne, toward earth" (516). They would instead have understood it as the claim that Israel's great hope was about to be realized within history, namely, that this present evil age was about to end. That hope would have been intertwined with their memory of what YHWH had done in the past and with their analysis of Israel's present situation.

Israel remembered its deliverance by YHWH from slave labor in Egypt and its entrance into the promised land. It remembered the founding of the Davidic monarchy. And it remembered the first Temple, built by Solomon, where YHWH had chosen to dwell. "The Psalms, which formed the staple diet of Jewish worship [during the time of the first Temple], continually celebrated the fact that Israel's god was Lord of the whole earth, and that he had chosen to dwell in the Temple in Jerusalem, whence he would hear his people's prayers and come to their aid" (205). The Temple, "in being YHWH's dwelling-place, was the spot where heaven and earth met" (205).

The destruction of the first Temple by the Babylonians, the end of Israel's self-rule, and its forced exile from the land were catastrophes of unspeakable dimensions. They could only be explained in terms of YHWH's abandonment of Israel. The glory of YHWH, the Shekinah, had departed from the Temple; the Davidic monarchy had been cast aside; and rather than protecting Israel from its enemies, YHWH had delivered Israel into the hands of its enemies, who then exiled it from the land of promise.

A remnant had returned from Babylon to live in the land of promise, and the Temple had been rebuilt. But Israel's longing was not yet requited. Its return from exile was incomplete; it remained subject to a foreign power; the Davidic monarchy had not been restored. Its enemies remained as powerful and menacing as ever. And YHWH had not returned to Zion "to deal with evil, to right wrongs, to bring justice to those who were thirsting for it like dying people in a desert" (172). Israel's identity, in its condition of quasi-exile, was thought by many to depend on faithfully keeping Torah.

Let me now quote Wright:

If [in this situation] someone were to speak to Jesus' contemporaries of YHWH's becoming king, we may safely assume that they would have had in mind, in some form or other, this two-sided story concerning the double reality of exile. Israel would "really" return from exile; YHWH would finally return to Zion. But if these were to happen there would have to be a third element as well: evil, usually in the form of Israel's enemies, must be defeated. Together these three themes form the metanarrative implicit in the language of the kingdom. . . . It cannot be stressed too strongly that the "kingdom of God" as a theme within second-Temple Judaism connoted first and foremost this complete story-line. (206)

Jesus Subverts the Traditional Understanding
of the Coming of the Kingdom of God

What I have presented thus far is Wright's exposition, stripped of its rich details, of what a "Jew-in-the-village in the first half of the first century" would have thought had a prophet come through proclaiming the coming of the kingdom of God. He would have thought that the prophet was predicting "the coming vindication of Israel, victory over the pagans, the eventual gift of peace, justice, and prosperity" (204).

But had he listened with any care to this particular prophet, Jesus of Nazareth, he would have discerned that there was much that was strange and unexpected about what the prophet was saying. Other people were coming through the village offering programs of liberation and renewal for Israel: some urged armed resistance to the Romans, some urged top-to-bottom reformation of the Temple cult, some urged more scrupulous observance of Torah. This prophet pronounced judgment on nationalist programs of armed resistance to Rome and declared that the day of the Temple cult and of Torah-observance was over.

He proclaimed the end of Israel's exile; but he was working with a different understanding of exile, and thus with a different understanding of how exile ends. He proclaimed vindication of Israel and victory over its enemies; but he was working with a different understanding of vindication and of victory. He proclaimed the return of YHWH to Israel; but he was working with a different understanding of YHWH's presence. In short, Jesus was employing Israel's traditional self-understanding in such a way as to subvert it. Let me again quote Wright:

> Jesus was announcing that the long-awaited kingdom of Israel's god was indeed coming to birth, but that it did not look like what had been imagined. The return from exile, the defeat of evil, and the return of YHWH to Zion were all coming about, but not in the way Israel had supposed. The time of restoration was at hand, and people of all sorts were summoned to share and enjoy it; but Israel was warned that her present ways of going about advancing the kingdom were thoroughly counter-productive, and would result in a great national disaster. (201)

Not only was Jesus announcing that the story of Israel was now coming to its decisive climax, albeit in unexpected ways. He indicated that it was coming to its decisive climax in his own words and works. "He believed that it was his own task not only to announce, but also to enact and embody, the three major kingdom-themes, namely, the return from exile, the defeat of evil, and the return of YHWH to Zion" (481). "He saw himself, not just as one prophet among many, . . . but as the prophet through whose work Israel's history would finally reach its climactic moment" (196). His "beliefs were those of a first-century Jew *who believed that the kingdom was coming in and through his own work*. His loyalty to Israel's cherished beliefs therefore took the form of critique and renovation from within; of challenge to traditions and institutions whose true purpose, he believed (like prophets long before, and radicals in his own day), had been grievously corrupted and distorted; and of new proposals which, though without precedent, were never mere innovation" (652).

All too briefly then: what was Jesus saying, and what did he see himself as doing? As their opening summary of Jesus' proclamation, both Matthew and Mark report Jesus as saying, "Repent, for the kingdom of God is at hand" (Matt. 4:17; Mark 1:15). In thus connecting the coming of the kingdom with repentance, Jesus was saying nothing new. Every faithful Jew of the time believed that it was because of its disobedience that God had allowed Israel's exile and that "a once-for-all national repentance . . . would be necessary for the exile to end at last" (251) and for YHWH once again to dwell with his people. What was new in Jesus' call for repentance was not the call as such but his message as to the fundamental sins of which Israel had to repent.

Israel had to repent of its "idolatrous nationalism" (331). Israel was being led to ruin by its zealous defense and practice of "those aspects of Torah which marked out Israel over against [its] pagan neighbors" (385): "the Temple cult, and the observance of sabbaths, of food taboos, and of circumcision" (384). Instead of being a light to the nations as it was called to be, Israel was using Temple and Torah "as a defence against Gentiles and hence as a reinforcement of national boundaries and aspirations" (389). "It was time to relativize those god-given markers of Israel's distinctiveness" (389). And as to the Temple itself, which was "the central symbol of the whole national life, [it] was under divine threat, and, unless Israel repented, it would fall to pagans" (417). The Temple had become a den of brigands, and the Temple cult "so horribly compromised that the only solution was for it to be destroyed" (353). It had "become hopelessly corrupt, . . . as ripe for judgment as it had been in the days of Jeremiah" (317).

Israel also had to repent of its long tradition of "holy war" (448-49) and its tendency to resort to armed violence in defense of the nation. Jesus' "challenge to Israel [was] aimed precisely at telling Israel to repent of her militaristic nationalism. Her aspirations for national liberation from Rome, to be won through a great actual battle, were themselves the tell-tale symptom of her basic disease, and had to be rooted out. Jesus was offering a different way of liberation, a way which affirmed the humanness of the national enemy *as well as* the destiny of Israel, and hence also affirmed the destiny of Israel as the bringer of light to the world, not as the one who would crush the world with military zeal" (450). In parables and sayings "Jesus consistently and continually warned his contemporaries that unless Israel repented . . . , i.e. gave up her militant confrontation with Rome and followed his radical alternative vision of the kingdom — then her time was up. Wrath would come upon her, in the form not so much of fire and brimstone from heaven as of Roman swords and falling stonework" (317).

Indeed, so prominent in his prophetic ministry was Jesus' prediction of the destruction of Jerusalem and the Temple, unless Israel changed her ways, that his reputation as a prophet was staked "on his prediction of the Temple's fall within a generation." If "the Temple remained for ever, and his movement fizzled out . . . , he would be shown to have been a charlatan, a false prophet, maybe even a blasphemer. But if the Temple was to be destroyed and the sacrifices stopped; if the pagan hordes were to tear it down stone by stone; and if his followers [were to] escape from the conflagration unharmed, in a re-enactment of Israel's escape from their exile in doomed Babylon — why, then he would be vindicated, not only as a prophet, but as Israel's representative" (362). If "Jerusalem is destroyed, and Jesus' people escape from the ruin just in time, *that will be* YHWH becoming king, bringing about the liberation of his true covenant people, the true return from exile, the beginning of the new world order" (364).

Israel's true exile lay not in the fact that, though living in the land of promise, it remained subject to a foreign power. Its true exile lay in the fact that its way of life alienated it from God. Return from exile required the repentance of rooting out its idolatrous nationalism and its tendency toward violence and living an entirely new way of life, a new *praxis:* love of the neighbor, whoever the neighbor may be, even if the neighbor is an enemy, offering forgiveness rather than seeking vengeance, pursuing justice for the poor, the downtrodden, and the vulnerable, sharing meals with religious and social outcasts, showing no partiality. The call to repentance "was a *political* call, summoning Israel as a nation to abandon one set of agendas and embrace another" (251).

It must not be overlooked that repentance, for Jesus, "did not involve going to the Temple and offering sacrifice" (257). The day of the Temple cult and its sacrifices was over. His summons was radical. "It had nothing to do with urging people to visit the Temple more frequently, to offer more sacrifices, to take more care over ritual purification. . . . His implied narrative continued, not with national restoration *per se* (as one might have expected from within the normal Jewish story) but with the challenge to his [band of] hearers to follow a different way of being Israel, and to await a different sort of vindication" (258).

"The time is fulfilled, and the kingdom of God is at hand," Mark reports Jesus as saying; "repent and believe in the gospel" (1:15). Faith was a central component of the new way of being Israel that Jesus was urging. Faith in what? Faith in Jesus himself. "The 'faith' which is the concomitant of so many of [Jesus'] acts of healing is not simply 'believing that Israel's god can do this.' It is believing *that Israel's god is acting climactically in the career of Jesus himself.* Both halves of this are equally important: (a) this is the moment Israel has been expecting; (b) this moment is constituted and characterized precisely by the presence and activity of Jesus" (262).

And just as Jesus was not merely announcing the coming of the kingdom but bringing it about, so also those of his hearers who followed his summons were not just practicing a different way of being Israel but were themselves the true Israel. In their repentance, Israel's alienation from God, its exile, was ending. "The basic story Jesus was telling invited his hearers to see themselves as the true Israel, returning at last from exile, and turning back to their God as an essential part of the process" (256). Jesus was summoning his hearers to *be* Israel in a new way, to take up their roles in the unfolding drama; and he assured them that, if they followed him in this way, they would be vindicated when the great day came. In the course of all this he was launching a decisive battle with the real satanic enemy — a different battle, and a different enemy, from those Israel had envisaged" (201).

Israel had to repent of its exclusivistic nationalism and of the vengeful violence that so often went along with it. But neither of these was the root of the problem. "Jesus' analysis of the plight of Israel went beyond the specifics of behaviour and belief to what he saw as the root of the problem: the Israel of his day had been duped by the accuser, the 'satan.' *That which was wrong with the rest of the world was wrong with Israel, too.* 'Evil' could not be located conveniently beyond Israel's borders, in the pagan hordes. It had taken up residence within the chosen people. The battle against evil — the correct analysis of the problem, and the correct answer to it — was therefore of a different order from that imagined by his contemporaries" (446-47). Throughout his career Jesus had been in combat with this strange evil force that haunted the world: that was the significance of the exorcisms, of the healings, of some of the controversies. The healings and the exorcisms were dramatic signs of victory over the evil force, signs of the coming of the kingdom and the restoration of creation.[5] Jesus went to Jerusalem in order to engage this strange evil force, which he had been combatting throughout his career, in the final and decisive battle, realizing that this final stage in the battle would involve suffering. For "suffering was itself a key ingredient within the Jewish expectation of the great deliverance, the great victory" (465). Jesus "took upon himself the totally and comprehensibly Jewish vocation not only of *critique* from within; not only of *opposition* from within; but of *suffering the consequences* of critique and opposition from within" (595). He "took upon himself the 'wrath' which was coming upon Israel *because she had refused his way of peace*" (596). "Israel was in exile, suffering at the hands of the pagans; the Roman cross was the bitterest symbol of that ongoing exilic state. He would go ahead of his people, to take upon himself both the fate that they had suffered one way or another for half a millennium at the hands of pagan empires and the fate that his contemporaries were apparently hell-bent upon pulling down on their own heads once for all" (596).

And how would the evil one be defeated? It "would be defeated, not by military victory, but by a *doubly* revolutionary method: turning the other cheek, going the second mile, the deeply subversive wisdom of taking up the cross. The agenda which Jesus mapped out for his followers was the agenda to which he himself was obedient. This was how the kingdom would come, how the battle would be won" (465). "All through his public career he had acted on the basis of compassion for the multitudes, for the poor, for the sheep without a shepherd. . . . The earliest Christians regarded Jesus' achievement on the cross as the decisive victory over evil. But they saw it, even more, as the climax of a career in which active, outgoing, healing love had become the trademark and hallmark" (607).

---

5. Cf. Wright, *How God Became King*, p. 195: "The exorcisms, in particular, are not simply the release from strange bondage of a few poor benighted souls. . . . For Jesus and the evangelists, they signalled something far deeper that was going on, namely, the real battle of the ministry, which was not a round of fierce debates with the keepers of orthodoxy, but head-on war with the satan."

The Early Christian Reworking

You and I live after the two great events in which Jesus and his proclamation were vindicated: the resurrection of Jesus and the destruction of
Jerusalem and the Temple. Those two events, especially the former, led
the early church to see itself as living in the new age that Jesus had pre-
dicted and brought about. In this new age they did not abandon the idea
of the kingdom of God as outdated, nor did they use language about the
kingdom of God to refer to something totally different from what Jesus
meant. Instead they reworked the idea so that it would fit their new situation. "The symbolic world of first-century Judaism [was] rethought from
top to bottom, even while its underlying theology (monotheism, election,
and eschatology) [was] explicitly retained" (218). Wright highlights two
elements in the reworking.

First, early Christian kingdom-language, as we find it in the episto-
lary literature of the New Testament and in the book of Acts, "has little
or nothing to do with the vindication of ethnic Israel, the overthrow of
Roman rule in Palestine, the building of a new Temple on Mount Zion,
the establishment of Torah-observance, or the nations flocking to Mount
Zion to be judged and/or to be educated in the knowledge of YHWH"
(219). "The story of the new movement is told without reference to the
national, racial, or geographical liberation of Israel" (218). "The regular
Jewish symbols are completely missing" (218). And "the *praxis* of the kingdom (holiness) is defined without reference to Torah" (218). The writers
do not speak "of Israel and her national hope" but instead "of a redeemed
humanity and cosmos" (218). They see themselves as living at "the time
when the covenant purpose of the creator, which always envisaged the
redemption of the whole world, has moved beyond the narrow confines of
a single race (for which national symbols were of course appropriate), and
called into being a trans-national and trans-cultural community. Further,
[they see themselves as living at] the time when the creator, the covenant
god himself, has returned to dwell with his people, but not in a Temple
made with hands" (219).

Second, the kingdom is now referred to as belonging not only to
the true god but to Jesus, the Messiah. And in an important Pauline passage, this joint kingdom of the creator god and of the Messiah is described
in chronological terms. The Messiah must reign, says Paul, "until he has
put all his enemies under his feet. Death is the last great enemy to be destroyed." "Then comes the end, when the Messiah hands over the kingdom

to the god who is the father, when he shall have suppressed all rule and all authority and power."[6]

Paul's point, says Wright, is that "the creator god is completing, through the Messiah, the purpose for which the covenant was instituted, namely, dealing with sin and death, and is thereby restoring creation under the wise rule of the renewed human being. The vital difference between this view and those we find in non-Christian second-Temple literature is that the kingdom is in a sense already present, as well as in another sense still future. . . . [T]he 'kingdom of the Messiah' is already established, while the 'kingdom of God', in this stricter sense, is yet to come. We see here exactly that tension between present realization and future hope which is so utterly characteristic of early Christianity as a whole and so puzzlingly opaque to generations of modern scholars. . . . What we find across the board in early Christianity . . . is a firm belief in the presentness of the kingdom, *alongside* an equally firm belief in its futurity, these two positions being held together within a refined apocalyptic scheme" (216-17). "The point of the present kingdom is that it is the first-fruits of the future kingdom; and the future kingdom involves the abolition, not of space, time, or the cosmos itself, but rather of that which threatens space, time, and creation, namely, sin and death" (218).

Back to Where We Began

The question I posed was, what are we asking God to do when we ask God to hear favorably our address to God? How are we to understand this liturgical act? I suggested that all our petitions should be understood as having, as their overarching context, our prayer for the coming of God's kingdom. And that led us into an extensive discussion, under the guidance of N. T. Wright, of God's kingdom and its coming.

We who are Christians long for the coming of God's kingdom. Our longing does not remain on the level of the general and the abstract; it takes the concrete form of longing that the coming of God's kingdom include Ruth's healing, include the downfall of our tyrannical regime, include peace in the Middle East, and so forth. When we ask God to accept our prayers, we are asking God to accept our concrete longing for the coming of God's kingdom.

---

6. 1 Cor. 15:24-26. Wright's translation, in *Jesus and the Victory of God*, p. 216.

Of course if we, in our daily lives, are not playing our own role in the coming of God's kingdom, if we are not promoting the hallowing of God's name in our community, not promoting the doing of God's will in our nation, not working to the end that everybody has sustenance adequate for his or her daily life, not promoting release from the grip of one and another 'ism,' then our prayer is deviant, malformed. That's what we learn from the prophetic critique of Israel's rituals.

Can we say that we call to God's attention the ways in which our world falls short of the full manifestation of God's kingdom? Can we say that we remind God of these shortfalls? Yes, I think we can, provided that we understand ourselves, in doing so, as using our terms "remind" and "call to God's attention" with analogical extension.

Suppose that, in the context of declaring that the kingdom is God's and praying for the coming of the kingdom, we name Ruth's disease, name our tyrannical regime, name conflict in the Middle East, as indications of the kingdom's not yet having fully come, and pray that the coming of the kingdom may take the form of Ruth being healed, the form of our tyrannical regime being overthrown, the form of peace coming to the Middle East. If Ruth is healed, if the tyrannical regime is overthrown, if peace does come to the Middle East, we then receive these as signs and samples of the coming of the kingdom and we give God thanks and praise.

But suppose, on the other hand, that Ruth is not healed, that our regime is not overthrown, that peace does not come to the Middle East. How do we interpret that? Do we interpret that as God not having heard favorably our prayer for the coming of his kingdom?

We do not. We know that the coming of God's kingdom is slow, painfully slow; for reasons we do not understand, it takes time. The fact that sickness, oppression, and conflict remain is not for us a sign that God's kingdom is not coming. What we acknowledge is that our longing that a sign of the coming of the kingdom be Ruth's healing has not been fulfilled, that our longing that a sign of the coming of the kingdom be the overthrow of the regime has not been fulfilled, that our longing that a sign of the coming of the kingdom be peace in the Middle East has not been fulfilled. Living with unfulfilled longings of these sorts is intrinsic to the Christian life in this present age. God desires such longings.

Not only should our petition that God hear favorably our plea for forgiveness and our intercessions be set and understood within the frame of longing for the coming of God's kingdom; our prayer that God accept our praise and thanksgiving should likewise be set and understood within that frame. Praise and thanksgiving are themselves signs of the kingdom.

What's Implicit?

The liturgical theological question before us in this chapter has been, what is the understanding of God implicit in our liturgical acts of asking God to hear favorably our praise and thanksgiving, our plea for forgiveness, our supplications? The answer is now obvious: we understand God, unsurpassable in glory, holiness, and love, as engaged in bringing about the full manifestation of God's kingdom. In what we do in our daily lives, and in our enactment of the liturgy, we align ourselves with God's bringing about of God's kingdom; in our prayer, that God hear favorably what we say, we give voice to our longing for the coming of God's kingdom.

CHAPTER EIGHT

God as One Who Speaks

We have spent three chapters reflecting on the understanding of God implicit in our liturgical acts of addressing God. God, so I have argued, is implicitly understood in these acts as listening to us and hearing favorably what we say, doing so in the course of bringing about God's kingdom. It's time that we turn our attention to the other main type of liturgical action.

In the enactment of almost all liturgies the people do a good deal of listening to what is said to them; in the enactment of some Protestant liturgies they do little else. That a good deal of the enactment of a liturgy consists of the congregants listening to what is said to them is not immediately evident from the printed script for a traditional liturgy. Extended listening occurs when the sermon is preached. But usually all one finds in the printed script for the liturgy is the rubric "Sermon" or "Homily."

When the congregants listen to what is said to them they are, obviously, listening to what is said by one of their fellow human beings: their priest, their minister, a reader of Scripture, a leader for the prayers. But in Chapter Four I referred to a tradition of liturgical theology which holds that in a good many of our liturgical acts of listening we are listening to what God said or says to us by way of what some human being says. As an example of the point I cited the discussion of the matter by the Swiss liturgical scholar, J.-J. von Allmen. "All Christians agree," says von Allmen, "that the Word of God is an essential constituent of Christian worship. Without it, the cult would not be a living effective encounter between God and His people, but a mere human monologue or dialogue. It would not be a miracle, but rather a blind groping, longing and despair. . . . [T]he cult would be emptied of its substance and indistinguishable from a non-Christian cult."[1]

Recall that von Allmen distinguished three basic ways in which the Word of God is proclaimed in the liturgy: there is the proclamation that occurs when Scripture is read, the proclamation that occurs when the sermon is preached, and the proclamation that occurs when the minister pronounces the opening greeting, the absolution, and the closing benediction. Von Allmen calls these, respectively, *anagnostic* proclamation, *prophetic* proclamation, and *clerical* proclamation.

Von Allmen is surely mistaken in saying that all Christians agree that an enactment of the liturgy is "a living effective encounter between God and His people" by virtue of our listening to what God says to us in these various forms of proclamation. Perhaps all liturgical scholars agree on this. But surely not all Christians agree; indeed, it can safely be said that *most* Christians in the contemporary world do not. They believe that when we perform some liturgical act of listening, we are listening to nothing more than what some fellow human being has to say about God, Christ, Scripture, love, forgiveness, and the like. So once again we are confronted with the fact that disagreement and controversy arise already in the first of the three stages that I distinguished in the formation of liturgical theology, the stage in which we try to determine just what is going on in some liturgical act.

I propose not entering that controversy on this occasion. Instead I shall assume that von Allmen is right: by way of the reading of Scripture, the preaching of the sermon, and the clerical pronouncement of the opening greeting, the absolution, and the closing benediction, God speaks to the people and they listen to what God said or says. In an enactment of the liturgy we address the God of unsurpassable greatness who is bringing about God's kingdom, and God stoops down to listen to us and to hear favorably what we say. God also stoops down to speak to us, and we listen to what God says. The understanding of God implicit in the liturgy is that God is one who both listens and speaks.

But how are we to understand this idea of God speaking to us? That is the topic I will be wrestling with in this chapter. How can we best develop theologically the idea that God speaks to us in the liturgy? The topic of this chapter thus falls within the third of the three stages that I distinguished in

---

1. J.-J. von Allmen, *Worship: Its Theology and Practice* (London: Lutterworth Press, 1965), p. 13. Subsequent references to this volume will be made parenthetically in the text.

the formation of liturgical theology, the stage in which we give theological articulation to the understanding of God that we identify as implicit in the liturgy.

Two Understandings of God as Speaker

My strategy will be to present two quite different ways of developing the idea of God as one who speaks, in particular, as one who speaks in the enactment of the liturgy. On one way of developing the idea, the minister is a deputy of God. He or she speaks on behalf of God, in the name of God, so that his or her speaking counts as God here and now saying something to these particular people. This is Calvin's understanding of what happens in preaching. Speaking of the ecclesiastical office of minister he says that God "uses the ministry of men to declare openly his will to us by mouth, as a sort of delegated work, not by transferring to them his right and honor, but only that through their mouths he may do his own work — just as a workman uses a tool to do his work." God "declares his regard for us when from among men he takes some to serve as his ambassadors in the world, to be interpreters of his secret will and, in short, to represent his person" (*Institutes* IV.iii.1, p. 1053). Just a bit later Calvin refers to the minister as "a puny man risen from the dust [who] speaks in God's name" (IV.iii.1, p. 1054).

In one passage, von Allmen follows Calvin in speaking of the minister as an ambassador of God and as representing God (142). But this is an exception. In all other passages he speaks instead of the minister as *proclaiming the Word of God,* meaning by the "Word of God," Christ. The minister proclaims Christ.

About the clerical proclamation in general von Allmen says that "the minister, by means of a Biblical formula, declares and gives to the people the *greeting,* the *absolution* and the *blessing* of God" (138). This sentence, by itself, could be understood along Calvinist lines. But that von Allmen does not intend it to be so understood becomes clear a bit later when he asks, "What takes place in this 'clerical' proclamation of the Word of God, at the pronouncement of the greeting, the absolution and the blessing?" To this question his answer is, "Clearly, an event that is brought about by divine grace. The Word of God, perhaps even more than when it is proclaimed in an 'anagnostic' or 'prophetic' manner, comes into efficacious action with all the power of the divine RHEMA [i.e., Spirit]" (141). Nothing is said here about the minister functioning as an ambassador or representative of God. The minister proclaims Christ, the Word of God; and on the occasion of that proclamation the event occurs of Christ coming "into efficacious action" through the power of the Spirit.

About the blessing in particular von Allmen says that "it is the creative and efficacious Word of God which is then uttered and that is why those moments of the service when this Word resounds are especially fraught with spiritual power. The blessing is a word charged with power, in which God himself or a man representing Him transmits to persons, living beings or things, salvation, welfare, and the joy of living, and this same power is operative in the greeting and the absolution" (142).[2] Again, nothing is said about the minister functioning as an ambassador of God, nothing about the minister speaking on behalf of God. The minister utters the Word of God, that is, Christ; and on the occasion of that utterance the event occurs of God transmitting salvation to the listeners.

About the sermon von Allmen says that "in the hands of God, the sermon is a basic means by which there takes place a direct prophetic intervention in the life of the faithful and of the Church. . . . [Preaching] prevents the petrifaction of the Word of God in the *illic et tunc* of the event in which it was enshrined, of its coming in Jesus Christ, and makes that *illic et tunc* newly operative in the *hic et nunc*" (143). "Preaching is the prophetic word of the Church, mediating and guaranteeing the presence of Christ" (145). Notice, once again, that there is not even a hint of Calvin's idea of the minister as speaking in the name of God. As von Allmen sees it, in prophetic proclamation the minister proclaims Christ, the Word of God; and on that occasion the event occurs of Christ being present and "operative."

At the beginning of his discussion of church proclamation von Allmen remarks that "since we are dealing with liturgy and not systematic theology, I may be excused from including here a theology of the Word of God" (130-31). Be that as it may, there can be no doubt that in his understanding of how God speaks in the enactment of the liturgy, von Allmen is operating with a highly distinctive theology of God as speaker, namely, that of his fellow Swiss Reformed theologian, Karl Barth. Several times he explicitly refers to and quotes from Barth.

Von Allmen was not idiosyncratic on this point. Especially in Protestant circles Barth's development of the idea of God as speaker was and

---

2. I judge the clause "or a man representing Him" to be an error on von Allmen's part; it does not express his thought.

remains enormously influential. So we have to turn to Barth. Barth's theology of God as speaker is complex; it will take quite some time to get hold of just its basic contours.

Barth on Church Proclamation and the Word of God

Karl Barth was less sparing of words than any other theologian of the Christian church, with Hans Urs von Balthasar, his Catholic contemporary, not far behind. In the expansive two-volume Prolegomena to his massive *Church Dogmatics,* Barth developed his now-famous doctrine concerning the "threefold form" of the Word of God: the Word of God revealed in Jesus Christ, the Word of God written in Scripture, and the Word of God proclaimed in the church.[3] Our goal in what follows is to consider what Barth had to say about the Word of God as proclaimed in the church; but we cannot get there without first looking at what he had to say about the other two "forms" of the Word of God.

To turn to Barth's discussion of Jesus Christ as the Word of God after engaging N. T. Wright's presentation of the story told by the four gospels concerning Jesus and the victory of God is to be struck by several points of sharp contrast. It is to be struck, for one thing, by the extraordinary abstractness of Barth's discussion. We took note of Wright's observation that the Nicene and Apostles' creeds take us straight from incarnation to crucifixion, resurrection, and ascension; the creeds say nothing about the life of Jesus and of what he did and said. Barth, likewise, says almost nothing about the life of Jesus. And though the three events of crucifixion, resurrection, and ascension are indispensable components of Barth's teaching, they take distinctly second place to incarnation. At the center of Barth's discussion is "the fact that God's Word became a man and that this man has become God's Word" (I/2; 1).

What also strikes one is that the theme Wright identifies as the overarching theme in the gospels, that of God becoming king in Jesus the Messiah, plays a vanishingly small role in Barth's discussion. Barth's entire discussion is shaped instead by an idea that plays a minor role in Scripture

---

3. Karl Barth, *Church Dogmatics,* Volume I, Part 1: *The Doctrine of the Word of God,* trans. G. W. Bromiley (Edinburgh: T&T Clark, 1975); *Church Dogmatics,* Volume I, Part 2: *The Doctrine of the Word of God,* trans. G. T. Thomson and Harold Knight (Edinburgh: T&T Clark, 1956). Page references to these volumes will be incorporated into the text.

itself, namely, the idea of God revealing Godself. For Barth, the fundamental significance of the incarnation is that therein, and only therein, God is revealed. "God's revelation is Jesus Christ, the Son of God" (I/1; 137). "To say revelation is to say 'the Word became flesh'" (I/1; 118-19).

Lest there be any doubt as to what he means by "revelation," Barth explains that revelation is "the unveiling of what is veiled" (I/1; 118-19). In the incarnation God, who had previously been hidden from human beings, unveiled Godself by taking on our nature and dwelling among us. "The New Testament, like the Old Testament, is the witness to [this] revelation of the hidden God" (I/2; 106).

A concept of revelation that has often been employed in the Christian tradition and continues to be employed in some quarters is that of so-called "propositional revelation": God's revelation consists of God causing certain persons to believe certain propositions about God. Barth is abruptly dismissive of the idea. Revelation, he remarks, is not to be "dissolved . . . into a sum total of truths" which "are then propounded to us as truths of faith, salvation and revelation" (I/2; 507). Revelation is the revelation of God, not of some propositions about God. "The freely acting God Himself and alone is the truth of revelation" (I/1; 15). God's revelation is not to be compared to someone revealing some secrets about himself to another person but to someone revealing himself by coming out of concealment.

An obvious question to raise here is how Barth proposes to deal with the biblical declaration that the heavens declare the glory of God and that creation in general manifests God's wisdom, power, and fidelity. How does he deal with what I have called God's *creational glory?* Does he deny that God's glory is revealed in God's creation?

Contrary to what one would expect, nowhere in his extensive discussion of revelation in the two-volume Prolegomena does Barth discuss the matter. I think we can surmise, however, what he would say were the question put to him. Whereas the creation shows or manifests various attributes of God — God's glory, God's wisdom, God's power and fidelity — in Jesus Christ God's very self is revealed, not just some attributes of God. I take it that that is what Barth was getting at in the following passage: In the death of Jesus, God reveals "His divine person, His divine essence in distinction from the nature of divinity in general or the divine forms in which this is seen and reverenced. God Himself is needed to reveal this work, and especially to reveal Himself, His divine person and essence. Who but God could or would reveal God?" (IV/3.1; 412).

"Revelation is no more and no less than the life of God himself turned to us" (I/2; 483).[4]

If this is in fact what Barth would say, my response is that though there is indeed a distinction to be drawn between various attributes of God being revealed in creation and God himself being revealed in Jesus Christ, to draw the distinction is not to justify limiting the application of the term "revelation" to the latter; even less is it to justify neglect of the revelation of God in creation.

Back to what Barth has to say about Jesus Christ as God's revelation. In revealing Godself by becoming incarnate in Jesus Christ, God speaks, says Barth; God says something. Revelation, in this case, is also speech. Barth insists that "we have no reason not to take the concept of God's Word primarily in its literal sense. God's Word means that God speaks. Speaking is not a 'symbol' (as P. Tillich . . . thinks). It is not a designation and description which, on the basis of his own assessment of its symbolic force, man has chosen for something very different from, and quite alien to, this expression. . . . [T]he concept of the Word of God . . . means originally and irrevocably that God speaks" (I/1; 132-33).

What does God say in revealing Godself by becoming incarnate in Jesus Christ? God says, "God with us" (I/1; 160). Barth amplifies this crisp summary by distinguishing between what God says by way of command and what God says by way of promise. What God says by way of command is this: "God's word means in this context God's positive command . . . which lifts us up and controls us as a command that goes forth in a way we cannot foresee, and to which . . . we can only take up an attitude by repeating it as we think we have heard it and by trying to conform to it as well or

---

4. I thank Kevin Hector for making me aware that Barth's insistence that God is revealed only in Jesus Christ did not come out of the blue. Among Barth's most influential teachers was Wilhelm Hermann, who in turn was the greatest student of Albrecht Ritschl. In his essay "Theology and Metaphysics," Ritschl says this: "If one has experienced the fact that he knows God in Christ and only in Christ — and this fact arises from his existence within the Christian community that theology is to serve — then other revelations of God are, at the most, only of interest when one can measure them against the revelation that is mediated by the Son" (Albrecht Ritschl, *Three Essays,* trans. Philip Hefner [Eugene, OR: Wipf & Stock, 2006], p. 153). Though Barth would emphatically agree that one "knows God in Christ and only in Christ," I dare say that he would regard the rest of the sentence, after "then other revelations," as rather loosely stated. Ritschl claims that he is following Luther in the position that he states here. Whether or not he is correct about that, it's clear that in claiming that God is revealed only in Jesus Christ Barth was not an innovator but was continuing a line of thought that by his time was traditional in German theology.

badly as we can. . . . [It is] God's own direction" (I/1; 90). What God says by way of promise is this: "The promise given to the Church in this Word is the promise of God's mercy which is uttered in the person of Him who is very God and very Man and which takes up our cause when we could not help ourselves at all because of our enmity against God. The promise of this Word is thus Immanuel, God with us . . ." (I/1; 107-8).

Barth declares that God's promise is uttered *in the person* of the one who is very God and very Man.[5] He would say the same, of course, about God's command; it too is uttered *in the person* of the one who is very God and very Man. What is noteworthy about this declaration is that the words actually spoken by Jesus fall out of the picture. No doubt Barth believed that in Jesus of Nazareth speaking, God was speaking — not speaking *by way of* words spoken by someone other than God, but God himself speaking. Yet in his account of God speaking, Barth makes remarkably few references to what Jesus actually said; this is part of what makes for the extreme abstractness of his discussion. For Barth, God speaks primarily in *the person* of Jesus Christ, that is, in and by the incarnation *as such*. In one passage he says about Jesus: "In a way different from Israel's prophets He is not there to receive and transmit the Word of the Lord, but He speaks Himself, in fact He is this Word. He accomplishes a plenipotentiary representation of God in which God Himself is the witness for man" (I/2; 105).

The Word of God in Scripture

Let's move on to the second of the three forms of the Word of God. Unlike those who saw and heard Jesus in the flesh, you and I have no direct access to that speech of God which is God's self-revelation in Jesus Christ; our access is indirect, mediated by Scripture. The overarching category that Barth uses for the prophets of the Old Testament and the apostles of the New Testament is that of *witness;* they were witnesses to Jesus Christ, the Word of God. Witnessing, he says, "means pointing in a specific direction beyond the self and on to another. Witnessing is . . . the service which consists in referring to this other. This service is constitutive for the concept of the prophet and also for that of the apostle" (I/1; 111). The Old Testament

5. Cf. I/1; 107: "The prophetic and apostolic word is the word, witness, proclamation and preaching of Jesus Christ. The promise given to the Church in this Word is the promise of God's mercy which is uttered in the person of Him who is very God and very Man."

is the written deposit of the prophetic witnesses; the New Testament is the written deposit of the apostolic witnesses.

A number of things deserve to be emphasized here. First, as Barth repeatedly insists, the written deposit of a witness to revelation is not itself the revelation; the Bible is not God's revelation. "A real witness is not identical with that to which it witnesses, but it sets it before us" (I/12; 463). "In the Bible we meet with human words written in human speech, and in these words, and therefore by means of them, we hear of the lordship of the triune God. Therefore when we have to do with the Bible, we have to do primarily with this means, with these words, with the witness which as such is not itself revelation, but only — and this is the limitation — the witness to it" (I/12; 463). If we are "to think of the Bible as a real witness of divine revelation, then clearly we have to keep two things constantly before us and give them their due weight: the limitation and the positive element, its distinctiveness from revelation, in so far as it is only a human word about it, and its unity with it, in so far as revelation is the basis, object, and content of this word" (I/12; 463).

Second, a witness is not a deputy. There is both a passive side and an active side to the prophetic and apostolic witness: having been witnesses *of* God's revelation in Jesus Christ, the prophets and apostles then become, in turn, witnesses *to* that revelation. Their words, in actively witnessing to that revelation, are purely human; they do not speak on behalf of God. Nobody speaks on behalf of God. Further, though the Holy Spirit superintends both the witnessing-of revelation by the prophets and apostles and their witnessing-to revelation, so that their words genuinely present God's revelation to us, the Spirit does not superintend their witnessing in such a way as to rub out all human particularity, nor to prevent all error. "The prophets and apostles as such, even in their office, even in their function as witnesses, even in the act of writing down their witness, were real, historical men guilty of error in their spoken and written word. . . . Every time we turn the Word of God into an infallible biblical word of man or the biblical word of man into an infallible Word of God we resist that which we ought never to resist, i.e., the truth of the miracle that here fallible men speak the Word of God in fallible human words" (I/2; 529). The scope of error extends even to the theological and ethical views of the biblical writers.

Third, there are visible signs of strain when Barth, having identified God's revelation with Jesus Christ, tries to fit not only the New Testament writers but also the Old Testament writers under the category of witnesses to revelation. We find him saying, for example, "Revelation in the Old

Testament is really the expectation of revelation or expected revelation" (I/2; 71). And in another passage, "The Old Testament covenant is the revelation of God as thus specially defined, in so far as, being so defined, it is expectation of the revelation of Jesus Christ" (I/2; 83). To expect some revelation is not to witness that revelation. I have no idea why Barth was determined to squeeze the prophets along with the apostles under the single category of *witness.*

Fourth, Barth has committed himself to the contestable claim that everything in Scripture, including the Wisdom literature, is to be read as part of a story, and that that story has a single story-line, namely, the story-line of redemption — the story first of Israel expecting the occurrence of God's revelation, then of the occurrence of that revelation, and finally of the church recollecting that occurrence.[6] The Bible is unified, Barth insists, not by a unified theology or worldview but by the fact that all its parts point, in one way or another, to Jesus Christ. "To understand the Bible from beginning to end, from verse to verse, is to understand how everything in it relates to this [*Deus dixit*] as its invisible-visible centre" (I/1; 116).

This claim, I say, is contestable. I am myself attracted to the alternative view that David Kelsey has worked out in his magisterial *Eccentric Existence,* namely, that in Scripture we find three independent but interacting story-lines as to how the triune God relates to all that is not God: the story-line of creation and preservation, the story-line of redemption, and the story-line of consummation.[7]

One more point of exposition is necessary before we can move on to what Barth has to say about church proclamation. Barth is emphatic in his insistence that the Bible is not God's Word; Jesus Christ and Jesus Christ alone is God's Word, God's speech. Had the prophets and apostles been deputized to speak on behalf of God, then in the deposit of their speech we would discern what God said to those whom the prophets addressed. But they were not deputies. They were no more than witnesses to what God said; and God speaks only in Jesus Christ. God speaks by way of a human being only if God is that human being.

But Barth wishes to say something more about the relation of the Bible to the Word of God than that it is the deposit of those who were witnesses of, and witnesses to, the Word of God, that is, Christ. He says

---

6. "Expectation" and "recollection" are Barth's words; see I/2, §14.

7. David Kelsey, *Eccentric Existence: A Theological Anthropology* (Louisville: Westminster John Knox Press, 2009).

that now and then, here and there, the Bible "becomes God's Word." It becomes God's Word "to the extent that God causes it to be His Word, to the extent that He speaks through it." The Bible "becomes God's Word in this event; and in the statement that the Bible is God's Word the little word 'is' refers to its being in this becoming." The little word "is" does not refer to identity; the Bible is not identical with God's Word. Whether now and then, here and there, it becomes God's Word is "God's decision and not ours" (I/1; 109-110).

What is Barth getting at when he says that now and then, here and there, God speaks to us through the Bible and that, in that event, the Bible becomes God's Word? In another passage Barth says of the Bible itself that now and then, here and there, it speaks to us. "The presence of the Word of God itself, the real and present speaking and hearing of it, is not identical with the existence of the book as such. But in this presence something takes place in and with the book for which the book as such does indeed give the possibility, but the reality of which cannot be anticipated or replaced by the existence of the book. A free divine decision is made. It then comes about that the Bible, the Bible *in concreto,* this or that biblical context, i.e., the Bible as it comes to us in this or that specific measure, is taken and used as an instrument in the hand of God, i.e., it speaks to and is heard by us as the authentic witness to divine revelation and is therefore present as the Word of God" (I/2; 530).

I suggest that when Barth says that now and then, here and there, the Bible speaks to us, he means the same as when he says that God now and then speaks to us through the Bible. And what he means by that becomes clear in the following passages. For "men acquainted with God's Word through revelation, Scripture and proclamation, God's Word can and must become true in such a way that its truth becomes their own and they become responsible witnesses to its truth" (I/1; 214). They must be "determined by the Word of God in their existence, i.e., in the totality of their self-determination" (I/1; 214). Their relation to revelation must become "the relation of acknowledgment" (I/1; 214). "The man who so hears [the Bible] that he grasps and accepts its promise, believes. And this grasping and accepting of the promise: Immanuel with us sinners, in the word of the prophets and apostles, this is the faith of the Church" (I/1; 108; cf. I/1 160, 214, 230). "Faith in the promise of the prophetic and apostolic word, or better, the self-imposing of the Bible in virtue of its content . . . is . . . an event, and is to be understood only as an event. In this event the Bible is God's Word" (I/1; 109).

In short, when Barth says that now and then, here and there, God speaks to us through the Bible, he does not mean that on those occasions God says to us something in addition to what God has already said in Jesus Christ. He means that now and then upon the reading of the Bible God evokes in us faith in the one to whom the Bible witnesses, namely, Jesus Christ, the Word of God. And when he says that on occasion the Bible *becomes* the Word of God, he means the same thing.

The Word of God Preached

We are now, at last, in the position of being able to consider what Barth says about the "third form" of the Word of God, namely, the Word of God as preached in the church. The present-day preacher stands in a line of succession with the ancient prophets and apostles; one and all they present or point to Jesus Christ. What makes the succession possible, as we have seen, is Holy Scripture, "the deposit of what was once proclamation by human lips" (I/1; 201). "The Church can say anything at all about the event of God and man only because something unique has taken place between God and these specific men [who were witnesses], and because in what they wrote, or what was written by them, they confront us as living documents of that unique event" (I/2; 486).

But though the present-day preacher is to be set with the prophets and the apostles "initially under a single genus, . . . Jeremiah and Paul at the beginning and the modern preacher of the Gospel at the end of one and the same series" (I/1; 102), the role of the present-day preacher in that series is decisively different from that of the prophets and apostles. The role of the prophets and apostles is primary: they were witnesses of the revelation. The role of the preacher is secondary: his or her presentation of Jesus Christ is dependent on, and governed by, their witness.

"Christian preaching is speaking about God in the name of Jesus Christ. It is a human activity like any other" (I/2; 758). On the basis of the witness of the prophets and apostles it both points back to the Word of God and points forward to the future coming of the Word of God. In the former of these functions it is repetition. "[T]he discharge of preaching cannot be God's own Word as such but only the repetition of His promise, repetition of the promise: 'Lo, I am with you always!'" (I/1; 58-59).

But more takes place in authentic preaching than the human activities of recollecting and pointing forward to Jesus Christ, the Word of God.

What also takes place is "the self-proclamation of the Word of God" (I/2; 759). Preachers "in all their humanity are invited to share in God's own work of proclaiming His Word" (I/2; 757). "God commits Himself with His eternal Word to the preaching of the Christian Church in such a way that this preaching is not merely a proclamation of human ideas and convictions but, like the existence of Jesus Christ Himself, like the testimony of the prophets and apostles on which it is founded and by which it lives, it is God's own proclamation" (I/2; 745-46). It does not happen automatically that "when the Church speaks of God, God Himself will and does speak of Himself" (I/2; 759). "When human talk about God is for us not just that, but also and primarily and decisively God's own speech," that is a miracle (I/1; 93).

"The miracle of real proclamation does not consist in the fact that the willing and doing of proclaiming man with all its conditioning and in all its problems is set aside, that in some way a disappearance takes place and a gap arises in the reality of nature, and that in some way there steps into this gap naked divine reality" (I/1; 94). No; the miracle consists in the fact that by means of the human words of the preacher, "God speaks about Himself" (I/1; 95). "When the Church speaks of God, God Himself will and does speak of Himself" (I/2; 759). That last sentence makes it sound as if the speech of the preacher is merely the occasion of God's speaking; it is clearly Barth's view that it is not only the occasion but, as he sometimes calls it, the "instrument."

I know of no place in which Barth explains what he has in mind when he speaks of the divine self-proclamation that occurs by means of the preacher's speech. However, I think it is almost certain that he means the same thing as what he means when he says that God speaks to us through the Bible. He does not mean that God says something new and different from what God has already said in Jesus Christ. He means that God uses the preacher's speech to evoke in us faith in the one to whom the preacher points, namely, Jesus Christ, the Word of God. Recall that he says of the Bible that "it must continually become God's Word." He says the same thing of church proclamation; it too "must continually become God's Word" (I/1; 117). To become the Word of God is for listeners to be "determined by the Word of God [i.e., Jesus Christ] in their existence, i.e., in the totality of their self-determination" (I/1; 214).

Who Is Right — Calvin or Barth?

Let us review where we are in our discussion. I observed that in the enactment of almost all Christian liturgies, the people do a good deal of listening to what is said to them. I then said that the idea I wanted to explore was the idea, common among liturgical scholars, that in much of this listening, the people are not only listening to the words of some human being but listening to what God said or says to them. God is implicitly understood as one who speaks to the people in the enactment of the liturgy. The question I posed for this chapter was how to articulate theologically this understanding of God.

I pointed to Calvin as someone who held that, in church proclamation, the minister speaks in God's name, speaks on behalf of God. The minister is an ambassador of God, a deputy, a representative. I am not aware of any place in which Calvin develops the idea. In the course of his discussion of the Eucharist Calvin notes that yet something more takes place in the sermon than that God speaks to the congregants by way of the preacher's words; Christ, he says, *offers* himself to them. I will save my discussion of this additional dimension of the sermon for the next chapter.

After taking note of Calvin's understanding of church proclamation, I went on to note that we find a very different understanding of church proclamation in the twentieth-century liturgical scholar J.-J. von Allmen, even though, as a minister in the Swiss Reformed Church, von Allmen stood in the tradition of which Calvin was one of the founders. Rather than saying that the minister speaks on behalf of God, or in the name of God, von Allmen describes the minister as proclaiming the Word of God, the Word of God being Christ. Von Allmen declined to develop this idea on the ground that his topic was not theology but liturgy. There can be no doubt, however, that his understanding of God speaking was shaped by the theology of Karl Barth. Between von Allmen and John Calvin there stands Karl Barth. So we turned to Barth, with the aim of discovering Barth's understanding of God as speaker.

The systematic sweep and intricacy of Barth's proposal, and its theological boldness, are extraordinary. Here is Barth's view, now stripped to the bones: Jesus Christ is the Word of God; there is no other word of God than the word spoken in Jesus Christ. In church proclamation the preacher, on the basis of Scripture, presents to the congregants that Word of God, namely, Jesus Christ. The preacher does not speak *on behalf of* God; conversely, God does not speak *by way of* the preacher's speech. No one speaks on behalf of God. In the speech of Jesus of Nazareth, God spoke. But Jesus did not speak on behalf of God; Jesus was God. The action of the preacher with respect to God speaking is purely presentational, purely ostensive. The preacher points to Jesus Christ, the Word of God.

However, if things go as they are meant to go, something else happens when the preacher proclaims Jesus Christ, the Word of God. The miracle occurs of the Word of God proclaiming itself by means of the preacher's speech. Though Barth does not explain what he means by this reference to divine self-proclamation, almost certainly what he means is that the Holy Spirit employs the preacher's proclamation of the Word of God to evoke in the congregants faith in Jesus Christ, the Word of God. Barth speaks of that event as the sermon "becoming" the Word of God (see I/1; 109, 118).

Notice, now, that on this view God does not literally speak (i.e., perform an illocutionary act) by way of the enactment of the liturgy, and we do not literally hear God speaking. To employ what someone says to *effect* something in someone is not to speak, that is, is not to perform an illocutionary act. Recall our discussion in Chapter Five of speaking. By enunciating the words "It's raining" I can assert that it's raining. The act of enunciating the words "It's raining" is not to be identified with the act of asserting that it's raining, since each of these can be performed without performing the other. In speech-act theory the former is standardly called a *locutionary* act, the latter, an *illocutionary* act. One performs the illocutionary act *by* performing the locutionary act. But the connection is not causal; the locutionary act does not cause the illocutionary act. The connection is the non-causal connection of *counting-as*. One's performance of the locutionary act *counts as* one's performance of the illocutionary act; enunciating the words "it's raining" counts as asserting that it is raining. God's effecting faith in the hearers by means of the words of the preacher is not the same as God's performing some illocutionary act of speaking to the hearers by way of the speech of the preacher.[8]

Though, in my view, it's a mark against the Barthian view that God does not literally speak by way of what the preacher says, I concede that it is not, by itself, a decisive mark. Perhaps there are good reasons for holding

8. Those familiar with speech-act theory will wonder whether God's effecting faith in the hearers by means of the words of the preacher is an example of what J. L. Austin called *perlocutionary effect*. The perlocutionary effect of some illocutionary (or locutionary) act is some change caused by that act. On Barth's view, it is not the preacher's speech-act that causes faith in the hearers but the Spirit, using that speech-act as means.

that in the enactment of the liturgy God does not perform any illocution-ary acts. In short, the question remains open: who is right, Calvin or Barth?

An initial issue to consider is whether the idea of a human being speaking on behalf of God is conceptually coherent. Is this even a possibil-ity? I hold that it is. In my book *Divine Discourse* I explored at considerable length the phenomenon of what I called "double-agency discourse," that is, the phenomenon of one person speaking on behalf of another. Though one will not find any discussion of double-agency discourse in standard speech-act theory, it is, nonetheless, a common phenomenon; ambassadors speak on behalf of their heads of state, lawyers speak on behalf of their clients, and so forth. After exploring the general phenomenon of double-agency discourse, I then went on to develop the idea of a human being speaking on behalf of God, and the correlative idea of God then speaking by way of the speech of that human being. I did not defend the claim that this does sometimes happen; I contented myself with defending the claim that it could happen. The Calvinist interpretation of liturgical proclamation can-not be ruled out on the ground that it is conceptually incoherent.

The theological conviction that shapes Barth's entire theology of God as speaker is that God's speech is confined to what God says in the person and words of Jesus Christ, an implication of this conviction being that no human being speaks on behalf of God except Jesus of Nazareth, who, of course, is God. In my presentation I did not mention any reason that Barth gives for that conviction. I did not do so because he gives no reason, at least none that I have been able to discover. The conviction functions in his discussion as an unquestioned, never defended, assumption. There are some vague intimations here and there to the effect that he thinks it would be an infringement on God's freedom were God to allow human beings to speak on behalf of God. But the vague intimations are never clearly stated and developed; and I, at least, do not see how they could be plausibly developed.

I find these claims biblically untenable, that what God says is con-fined to what God says in Jesus Christ, and that no human being speaks on behalf of God. The prophets are consistently presented in Scripture as speaking on behalf of God, in the name of God. Six times over the prophet Amos pronounces words of judgment on the nations surrounding Israel, each time prefacing his highly specific words of judgment with the phrase "Thus says the LORD." Then he turns to pronounce words of judgment on Israel and Judah, in each of these cases also prefacing his words of judg-ment with the phrase "Thus says the LORD." The prophet is presented not as a mere instrument of God's speaking but as speaking on behalf of God, in the name of God, so that, by way of the words of judgment spoken by the prophet, God pronounces judgment on the nations, on Israel, and on Judah. The *words* of judgment are spoken by the prophet; but by way of the prophet's enunciation of those words, God pronounces judgment. It is God who is judging the nations, Israel, and Judah, not the prophet.

We know how Barth would respond. The prophet is not speaking on behalf of God; conversely, God is not pronouncing judgments — highly specific judgments, I might add — on the nations, Israel, and Judah by way of the prophet's deliverance of words of judgment. Rather, the prophet is pointing to Jesus Christ, the Word of God.

Let me make two comments about this response. First, I find it extremely implausible to hold that the prophets were doing no more than pointing to the Messiah, the Messiah being Jesus Christ, the Word of God. It's true, of course, that the prophetic words spoken by Amos and the other prophets were uttered within the context of eschatological expectations concerning the coming of a messiah. But the contents of the judgments spoken by Amos and the other prophets are not to be identified with that eschatological context. In verse 13 of the first chapter of the Book of Amos we read,

> Thus says the LORD,
> "For three transgressions of the Ammonites,
>   and for four, I will not revoke the punishment,
> because they have ripped up women with child in Gilead,
>   that they might enlarge their border."

I do not see how this highly specific judgment pronounced by God on the Ammonites can be identified with what God says to all humanity in the incarnation. It is, of course, connected to what God says to all humanity in Jesus Christ; but it is not identical. I find Barth's interpretation to be a radical reduction of the concrete specificity of the prophetic proclamations.

Second, Barth does not take seriously the words of the prophet, "Thus says the LORD." The prophets have often been interpreted not as speaking on behalf of God but as delivering to their hearers convictions that God had planted in them. On this interpretation, the words of judgment pronounced by the prophets are to be understood as prefaced with the words, "Let me convey to you what God has communicated to me."

That is not substantially different from Barth's interpretation, according to which the prophet conveys to his hearers what God has led him to believe that God says in Jesus Christ.

In some cases the prophets did convey to their hearers what God had said to them. In those cases they were functioning as reporters of divine speech, functioning as publicists. But that's not the natural way of reading those bold words of Amos, "Thus says the LORD." Those who heard those words were not hearing a report of what God had previously said to Amos; they were hearing God then and there pronouncing judgment on them.

Of course the fact that Scripture presents the prophets — and also, I would argue, the apostles — as speaking on behalf of God and in the name of God does not imply that we should understand church proclamation along the same lines. That remains an open question. May it be that the phenomenon of human beings speaking on behalf of God was confined to the prophets and the apostles? Put the question like this: Barth holds that the present-day preacher should be understood as standing in the same line as the prophets and apostles; just as they pointed to Jesus Christ, the Word of God, so also the preacher points to Jesus Christ, the Word of God. Suppose we hold that the prophets and apostles did not merely point to Jesus Christ but spoke on behalf of God. Should we nonetheless embrace the Barthian view of church proclamation, that the present-day preacher points to Jesus Christ but does not speak on behalf of God? Should we embrace that sort of discrepancy between prophecy and preaching?

The basic issue, as I see it, is the following. In one passage Barth, after insisting that church proclamation is not some new word invented by the preacher but "repetition of the divine promise," adds that this repetition "cannot consist in the mere reading of Scripture or in repeating and paraphrasing the actual wording of the biblical witness. This can be only its presupposition" (I/1; 59). The preacher "must be ready to make the promise given to the Church intelligible in his own words to the men of his own time" (I/1; 59). Proclamation occupies "the middle space between the particular text in the context of the whole Bible and the particular situation of the changing moment" (I/1; 79).

So far, no problem. The preacher has to present Jesus Christ to the congregants in such a way that the divine promise comes through to them; and that requires of the preacher that he or she not just quote Scripture but "translate" into the language of the people listening. But then Barth goes on to say the following: "[W]herever and whenever God speaks to man its content is a *concretissimum*. God always has something specific to say to each man, something that applies to him and to him alone. The real content of God's speech or the real will of the [person speaking] of God is not in any sense, then, to be construed and reproduced by us as a general truth" (I/1; 140).[9]

The preacher is to go beyond presenting, in words that the listeners can grasp, the "general truth" spoken by God to humankind in general in Jesus Christ, namely, "God with us"; the preacher is to *apply* that general truth to the specific situations of the particular people before him or her. By means of the preacher doing that, God does the same. God says something specific to these particular people, that specific thing having the structure of being an application of what God says in Jesus Christ.

If Barth is to be taken as speaking strictly here, when he says that God says something specific to each person, if he is not to be interpreted as speaking loosely, then this does not fit with the rest of what he says about God speaking. If God says to a specific person how the Word of God applies to him or her in their specific situation, then God is then and there saying a new thing. The event of God's saying that new particular thing is obviously not identical with the event of the incarnation, nor is its content identical with the general thing that God says in the incarnation. An application of some generality to a specific situation is distinct from the generality of which it is the application.

Here is the issue: When the preacher repeats and summarizes Scripture, putting what the biblical writers said into terms that the congregation understands, we can interpret what he or she is doing as presenting what God said by way of the prophets and apostles. But suppose the preacher goes beyond repeating and summarizing what the prophets and apostles said; suppose the preacher applies what they said to the lives of the people in front of him or her. In this "going beyond," the preacher says something new.

Should the congregants regard this "going beyond" as the preacher now merely expressing his or her own opinion, that opinion to be taken seriously or not, as the case may be? Or should they regard it as God saying something to them by way of the preacher's speech? They need not — indeed, they *should* not — regard whatever the preacher says as something that God says; Calvin does not hesitate to point to the fallibility of preach-

---

9. Where I have "person speaking," the text has "speaking person." The words, "the speaking person of God" make no sense; I assume that "speaking" and "person" got transposed.

ers. But should they listen for what God is saying to them specifically by way of what the preacher says?

A good many of those who participate in the liturgy do regard the preacher's "going beyond" what Scripture explicitly says as the preacher simply expressing the preacher's own opinions. Annoyed by what the preacher says when applying Scripture to their lives, they tell the preacher to stick with preaching the gospel and stop inserting his or her personal opinions. It has to be conceded that this is an understandable response to a good many sermons!

My view is that, at this point, we should use Barth against Barth. Against the Barth who insists that God never says anything other than what God says to all humankind in Christ, namely, "God with us," we should use the Barth who says that "God always has something specific to say to each [human being], something that applies to [to that person and to that person] alone." Be it granted that this last comment occurs almost inadvertently in Barth's text. Often what occurs inadvertently in a text is revelatory of chinks and cracks in the big scheme that the author is seeking to impose.

In preceding chapters of this book I argued that implicit in the Christian liturgy is the understanding of God as one who listens to us when we address God in our enactment of the liturgy. I think it would be strange indeed if God listened to us when we confess the specific sins of our time and place but did not then, by way of the minister's speaking words of absolution, pronounce those same specific sins forgiven but only issued a general "God with us." God not only presently listens to us when we enact the liturgy; God also presently speaks to us by way of our enactment of the liturgy. Liturgy is the site of mutual address between God and God's people.

The God of unsurpassable greatness and excellence humbles himself and elevates us by listening to what we say to God in our enactment of the liturgy. That same God humbles himself and elevates us by consenting to being represented by a mere human being in our enactment of the liturgy, so that what that human being says counts as God here and now saying something to us.

CHAPTER NINE

The Understanding of God Implicit in the Eucharist

In Chapter Four of this volume we took note of the fact that the two types of actions most pervasive in the liturgy are actions of the people addressing God and actions of the people listening to what is said to them. In the chapter preceding this one I argued that some of the latter are to be understood as the people listening to what God is saying to them by way of what some human being says; what the human being says *counts as* God saying something. The enactment of the liturgy is thus the site of mutual address between God and the people, with both parties functioning as speakers and as listeners; that has been our topic for the preceding five chapters.

Though speaking and listening are prominent and pervasive in the Christian liturgy, we must resist the temptation to think of them as constituting the totality of liturgical actions. In the liturgy we sing, we close our eyes, we fold our hands, we raise our hands, we keep silence, we kneel, we bow, we stand, we process, we are sprinkled with water, we are immersed in water, we pass the peace to each other, we deposit money in baskets, we light candles, we eat bread and drink wine, and in some liturgical traditions we spit. Some of these actions can be interpreted as actions whereby we perform speech actions, that is, illocutionary actions; but I judge that not all of them can plausibly be so interpreted. I want now to develop this point, that liturgical actions go beyond speech actions, by looking at the understanding of God implicit in one of the high points of the liturgy, if not, indeed, *the* high point, namely, in our enactment of the Eucharist, or as it is often called by Protestants, The Lord's Supper.

Several times over, in talking about the project of liturgical theology, I have made the point that we must not assume that discerning what is going on in some liturgical action is easy and straightforward, and that the hard and controversial work begins when we try to make explicit the understanding of God implicit in that action and to articulate that understanding theologically. This is true especially for the Eucharist; here, especially, we are confronted with alternative and controversial understandings of what is going on. Theological controversy does not arise after we have analyzed what is taking place in our enactment of the Eucharist; the analysis is itself shaped by controversial theological claims.

Obviously this is not the place to present the major alternative analyses of the Eucharist that have been developed over the centuries and then to argue for one of them; that would require at least a book. What I shall do instead is select and present one analysis and elicit the understanding of God implicit in that analysis. Since I am a member of the Reformed tradition, the analysis I will present is that of the "father" of the Reformed tradition, namely, John Calvin. I judge that Calvin's analysis, more than any other major analysis of the Eucharist, has been afflicted by stereotyped descriptions that obscure what he actually thought and wrote.

The Eucharist as a Memorial

All traditional eucharistic liturgies begin with a narrative of what God has done, set within the context of a prayer to God of praise and thanksgiving — hence the term "Eucharist," from the Greek word for thanksgiving, *eucharistia*. In all of them this narrative prayer of praise and thanksgiving reaches its climax with a report of what Jesus said over the bread and the wine at his last supper with his disciples, slightly different words being used in different liturgies to express what Jesus said, all of them taken from the slightly different versions to be found in the three synoptic gospels and in Paul's First Letter to the Corinthians. Here is how Paul reports what Jesus did and said, it being the consensus of scholars that this is the earliest report we have:

> The Lord Jesus on the night when he was betrayed took a loaf of bread, and when he had given thanks, he broke it and said, "This is my body that is for you. Do this in remembrance of me." In the same way he took the cup also, after supper, saying, "This cup is the new covenant in my blood. Do this, as often as you drink it, in remembrance of me." (1 Cor. 11:23-25)[1]

1. The Greek phrase translated here by the NRSV as "in remembrance of" is *eis anamnēsin*. I prefer the translation "as a memorial of."

Here is how the Book of Common Prayer (Rite Two) reports what Jesus did and said:

> On the night he was handed over to suffering and death, our Lord Jesus Christ took bread; and when he had given thanks to you, he broke it, and gave it to his disciples, and said, "This is my Body, which is given for you. Do this for the remembrance of me."
>
> After supper he took the cup of wine; and when he had given thanks, he gave it to them, and said, "Drink this, all of you: This is my Blood of the New Covenant, which is shed for you and for many for the forgiveness of sins. Whenever you drink it, do this for the remembrance of me." (362-63)

And here is how the Orthodox Liturgy reports what Jesus did and said:

> The night he was handed over — or rather surrendered himself for the life of the world — he took bread in his holy, pure, and blameless hands and having given thanks, he blessed it, consecrated it, broke it, and offered it to his disciples and apostles saying, "Take, eat, this is my body which is broken for you, for the remission of sins." Likewise after supper he offered the cup saying, "Drink from this all of you; this is my blood, of the New Testament, which is shed for you and for many for the remission of sins." (47-49)

Paul reports Jesus as saying, over both the bread and the wine, that his disciples are to do this as a memorial *(eis anamnēsin)* of him; that is, they are to re-enact our Lord's last meal as a memorial of him.[2] The Episcopal liturgy, in the passage quoted, picks up this reference to memorial action, as do all other traditional liturgies with the exception of the Orthodox. We enact the Eucharist as a memorial of Jesus.

A full and adequate analysis of the Eucharist thus requires, as one of its salient components, that the Eucharist is a memorial meal. And

---

2. Luke reports Jesus as saying "do this as a memorial of me" only over the bread; Matthew and Mark do not report him as saying it over either the bread or the wine. Jesus' meal in the upper room was not itself a memorial meal, of course, since he was still alive; in saying "do this as a memorial of me" Jesus was looking ahead to re-enactments of his last meal. (Or, in light of the fact that relatively soon the practice arose among Christians of re-enacting Jesus' last meal, perhaps the reference to a memorial was an interpolation on the part of Luke and Paul, expressing their conviction that this is what Jesus desired.)

since doing something as a memorial is neither speaking nor listening, we would advance our discussion if we explored this aspect of the Eucharist and made explicit the understanding of God implicit therein. Calvin does not, however, make a big point of this dimension of the Eucharist; it's not central in his analysis. So on this occasion I propose saying nothing more about this dimension and focusing instead on matters central to his analysis.[3]

My Body and Blood for You

Paul reports Jesus as saying over the bread, "This is my body that is for you"; he does not report Jesus as using the "for you" locution over the wine. Matthew and Mark report Jesus as using the "for you" locution over the wine but not over the bread. Luke reports Jesus as using the "for you" locution over both the bread and the wine. The traditional liturgies all use some version of the "for you" locution over both the bread and the wine.

The relevance of this point for our purposes here is the following: most traditional interpretations of the Eucharist treat the words attributed to Jesus as if there were a full stop after "this is my body" and another full stop after "this is my blood"; this interpretation has contributed to generating the controversies over real presence, transubstantiation, and the like. On Calvin's interpretation, the full stops come after "for you": "this is my body *for you*"; "this is my blood *for you*." This interpretation is pivotal for Calvin's entire analysis of the Eucharist; he says in one place, "the very powerful and almost entire force of the Sacrament lies in these words: 'which is given for you,' 'which is shed for you'" (*Institutes* IV.xvii.3; 1362).

Equally important for Calvin's interpretation is the fact that Jesus did not just declare that his body and blood are "for you," referring in the first instance to his disciples. He invited them to take, eat, and drink; and they did in fact take, eat, and drink. I quote Calvin's compact paraphrase of Christ's words: "Take, eat, drink: this is my body, which is given for you; this is my blood, which is shed for forgiveness of sins" (IV.xvii.3; 1362). We exaggerate only slightly if we say that Calvin's entire analysis of the

---

3. I have discussed at length the idea of the Eucharist as a memorial in my essay "The Remembrance of Things (not) Past," in *Christian Philosophy,* ed. Thomas V. Flint (Notre Dame: Notre Dame University Press, 1990). Hereafter in this chapter, all references to Calvin's analysis of the Eucharist will be to the *Institutes* (trans. Ford Lewis Battles [Philadelphia: Westminster Press, 1960]), unless otherwise noted.

Eucharist is shaped by these initial interpretations and emphases, along with his acceptance of the traditional definition of a sacrament as effecting what it signifies.

Having reported the words spoken by Jesus over the bread and wine at his last meal with his disciples, the priest or minister then offers the bread to the congregants with some such words as "the body of Christ, the bread of heaven," and he or she offers the wine with some such words as "the blood of Christ, the cup of salvation"; the congregants then eat the bread and drink the wine. For Calvin, the central signifying phenomena in the Eucharist are these actions — not the bread and wine as such, but the presider's actions of offering bread and wine to the congregants and the congregants' actions of receiving and ingesting the bread and wine. Calvin affirms that the bread signifies (represents, stands for) Christ's body and that the wine signifies (represents, stands for) Christ's blood. But the bread and the wine do not possess their signifying functions independently; they possess them within the context of the signifying function of the presider's actions of offering bread and offering wine and the signifying function of the congregants' actions of eating the bread and drinking the wine.

Christ Offers Himself and We Partake

If the basic signifying phenomena in the Eucharist are the presider's actions of offering bread and wine and the congregants' actions of eating the bread and drinking the wine, then what is signified must likewise be actions. What are those signified actions? Given what he has said thus far, it's hard to see that Calvin could say anything other than what he does say. The presider's actions of offering bread and wine to the recipients signifies (represents) Christ's offering them his body and blood, and their receiving and ingesting the bread and wine signifies (represents) their receiving and partaking of Christ's body and blood.

Now recall that Calvin follows the tradition in understanding a sacrament as effecting what is signified; "God accomplishes within what the minister represents and attests by outward action" (*Institutes* IV.xiv.17; 1293). Thus the presider's actions of offering bread and wine do not merely signify for our "understanding and imagination" (IV.xxvii.11; 1379) that Christ has offered his body and blood for us. By way of the presider's offering of bread and wine to the congregants, Christ now does in fact offer his body and blood to them. "Our Lord gives us in the Supper what he signifies by it, and we thus really receive the body and blood of Jesus."[4]

So too, the congregants' actions of eating the bread and drinking the wine do not merely signify that they accept Christ's offer; by eating and drinking, "they really receive the body and blood of Christ." "There are some," says Calvin, "who define the eating of Christ's flesh and the drinking of his blood as, in one word, nothing but to believe in Christ." Calvin demurs. "It seems to me that Christ meant to teach something more definite, and more elevated, in that noble discourse in which he commends to us the eating of his flesh [John 6:26ff.]. It is that we are quickened by the true partaking of him, and he has therefore designated this partaking by the words 'eating' and 'drinking,' in order that no one should think that the life that we receive from him is received by mere knowledge. As it is not the seeing but the eating of bread that suffices to feed the body, so the soul must truly and deeply become partaker of Christ that it may be quickened to spiritual life by his power" (IV.xvii.5; 1365). Though it is not a condition of Christ's offering his body and blood to someone in the sacrament that that person have faith, it is a condition of genuinely *receiving* Christ's body and blood that she have faith.

In several of the preceding chapters in this volume I have employed the idea of one act counting as another — not *causing* another but *counting as* the other. One can assert that it's humid today by assertively uttering the English sentence "It's humid today." When one does so, one's act of uttering the English sentence *counts as* one's act of asserting that it's humid today. And in our discussion of God speaking in the preceding chapter I called attention to the phenomenon of double-agency discourse; sometimes one person says something by way of another person speaking on his behalf. In such a case, what the former person says *counts as* the latter person saying something.

What I did not take note of in my preceding chapters is that the phenomenon of one act counting as another is not limited to speaking; an example of the point is that turning one's back on someone may count as insulting the person. Neither did I take note of the fact that double-agency discourse is just one species of double-agency action in general; my lawyer's signing his name on a sheet of paper may count as my buying a house.

---

4. Calvin, "Short Treatise on the Lord's Supper," in *Calvin: Theological Treatises,* trans. J. K. S. Reid (Philadelphia: Westminster John Knox Press, 1954), p. 163. Every now and then Calvin speaks, as he does in the passage quoted, of God or Christ as doing the signifying. That is clearly an imprecise expression of his thought. It's the actions of the presider and the actions of the congregants that do the signifying.

I suggest that the general concept of one act counting as another, and the general concept of double-agency action, are helpful in formulating Calvin's analysis of the eucharistic actions. The presider's actions of offering the bread and wine to the congregants *count as* Christ's offering to them his body and blood for their partaking. The presider's actions do not merely symbolize Christ's offering of his body and blood, nor do they merely provide the occasion for Christ's offering; neither are they the means of Christ's offering, if one thinks of means in terms of causation. The presider's actions *count as* Christ's offering his body and blood for our partaking; this is how, in the Eucharist, Christ offers us his body and blood for our partaking. So too, our actions of taking the bread and eating it, and taking the wine and drinking it, *count as* our accepting Christ's offer and taking or receiving Christ's body and blood into ourselves. This is how, in the Eucharist, we accept Christ's offer of himself for our partaking. Our partaking of the bread and wine count as our partaking of Christ.

I observed that, for Calvin, the central signifying phenomena in the Eucharist are not the bread and wine as such but the presider's actions of offering bread and wine to the congregants and their actions of taking, eating, and drinking. Within the context of those signifying actions the bread and the wine do, however, play an indispensable role. And not only do they play an indispensable role. Though for Calvin it is of fundamental importance to note and keep in mind that the full sentences Jesus uttered were "This is my body *for you*" and "This is my blood *for you*," it remains the case that Jesus did say, referring to the bread, "This is my body," and that he did say, referring to the wine, "This is my blood." So what is the force of the "is" in these two sentences? And more generally, what is the role of the bread and the wine in the eucharistic actions?

The repetition by the presider of Jesus' words have traditionally been understood as words of consecration; the presider consecrates this ordinary bread and this ordinary wine to this special sacramental use. And traditional Catholicism has held that, on the occasion of the presider uttering these words of consecration, God transubstantiates the bread into Christ's body and the wine into Christ's blood, so that though it appears to be bread that the congregants are eating, it is not bread, and though it appears to be wine they are drinking, it is not wine.

Calvin's view is that the bread *signifies* Christ's body and that the wine *signifies* his blood. In support of this interpretation he quotes a sizable number of scriptural passages in which the copula "is" does not express identity but functions as a synonym of "signifies" (*Institutes* IV.xvii.21;

1385). On this interpretation, the presider's enunciation of the words of consecration are to be understood as *assigning signification* to the bread and the wine: "let this bread stand for (signify) Christ's body," "let this wine stand for (signify) Christ's blood." Whereupon, when the presider offers the consecrated bread to the congregants, the bread stands for Christ's body and the presider's offering of the bread counts as Christ offering his body, and when the presider offers the consecrated wine to the congregants, the wine stands for Christ's blood and the presider's offering the wine counts as Christ offering his blood.

Calvin offers an interesting argument against interpreting the "is" in Christ's words as the "is" of identity. Recall that he accepts the traditional understanding of a sacrament as effecting what is signified. Now if the bread is transubstantiated into the body of Christ and the wine into his blood, then there is no longer any bread and there is no longer any wine. And if there is no longer any bread or wine, then there is no longer anything that signifies. The doctrine of transubstantiation is incompatible with the traditional understanding of a sacrament as effecting what is signified. It's true that what is claimed to be the body of Christ *appears* to be bread and what is claimed to be the blood of Christ *appears* to be wine. But these are only appearances; there is no bread and there is no wine, and hence no signifiers. "Christ's purpose was to witness by the outward symbol that his flesh is food; if he had put forward only the empty appearance of bread and not true bread, where would be the analogy or comparison needed to lead us from the visible thing to the invisible? . . . The nature of the Sacrament is therefore cancelled, unless, in the mode of signifying, the earthly sign corresponds to the heavenly thing" (IV.xvii.14; 1376).

The word "corresponds" in that last sentence leads to an important additional point concerning Calvin's analysis. Often when we assign one thing to signify or stand for another our assignment is arbitrary, or very nearly so; we could just as well have assigned the signifying function to a large number of other things. Calvin rejects the idea that it is purely arbitrary that bread is assigned to stand for Christ's body and that wine is assigned to stand for his blood. In the context of defending his interpretation of the meaning of the copula in Christ's declaration he says this: "For though the symbol differs in essence from the thing signified (in that the latter is spiritual and heavenly, while the former is physical and visible), still, [it does] not only symbolize the thing that it has been consecrated to represent as a bare and empty token, but also truly exhibits it" (IV.xvii.21; 1385). He enlists Augustine in support: "If sacraments did not have a certain likeness to those things of which they are sacraments, they would not be sacraments at all. Moreover, from this likeness they often also take the names of the things themselves" (IV.xvii.21; 1386). "Let it therefore remain certain that in the Supper the flesh of Christ is not truly and fittingly promised to us to be truly food unless the true substance of the outward symbol corresponds to it" (IV.xvii.15; 1378).

Thus when Calvin attempts to describe partaking of Christ's body and blood, he does not apply some independently arrived at theory of partaking or participation. Instead, he is guided in his reflections by the thesis that it is by no means arbitrary that eating bread and drinking wine would be used to signify partaking of Christ's body and blood. The signifying action *depicts, pictures* the signified action. Accordingly, Calvin first reflects on the function in our lives of eating bread and drinking wine, and he then employs what he calls "the analogy of the sign" (IV.xvii.10; 1370) to understand what it is to partake of Christ's body and blood. He uses eating bread and drinking wine as a *model* for understanding partaking of Christ's body and blood. "Our souls are fed by the flesh and blood of Christ in the same way that bread and wine keep and sustain physical life" (IV.xvii.10; 1370). Or to put the same idea in yet different words: Calvin employs *just as . . . so also* reasoning to gain some understanding of what it is to partake of Christ's body and blood: "by true partaking of him, his life passes into us and is made ours — just as bread when taken as food imparts vigor to the body" (IV.xvii.5; 1365).

> From the physical things set forth in the Sacrament we are led by a sort of analogy to spiritual things. Thus, when bread is given as a symbol of Christ's body, we must at once grasp this comparison: as bread nourishes, sustains and keeps the life of our body, so Christ's body is the only food to invigorate and enliven our soul. When we see wine set forth as a symbol of blood, we must reflect on the benefits which wine imparts to the body, and so realize that the same are spiritually imparted to us by Christ's blood. These benefits are to nourish, refresh, strengthen, and gladden. For if we sufficiently consider what value we have received from the giving of that most holy body and the shedding of that blood, we shall clearly perceive that those qualities of bread and wine are, according to such analogy, excellently adapted to express those things when they are communicated to us. (IV.xvii.3; 1363)

In this passage Calvin speaks of the "benefits" of drinking wine, thereby implicitly distinguishing between partaking of (drinking) wine and the benefits of so doing; he likewise speaks of the "benefits" of partaking of Christ's blood, thereby implicitly drawing a contrast between partaking of Christ's blood and the benefits of so doing. He employs the same distinction in other passages. Though the contrast is not drawn emphatically, I suggest that it is important for understanding Calvin's thought.

By performing the actions of eating the bread and drinking the wine, we take or receive Christ into ourselves; we partake of Christ. Having thus partaken of Christ, received Christ into ourselves, then, by the power of the Spirit, Christ dwells and works within us for our justification, sanctification, and glorification; that's the benefit.[5] Here is one of several passages in which Calvin describes the benefits of our having received Christ into ourselves and of Christ now dwelling and working within is. The passage revels in paradox:

> This is the wonderful exchange which, out of his measureless benevolence, he has made with us; that, becoming Son of man with us, he has made us sons of God with him; that, by his descent to earth, he has prepared an ascent to heaven for us; that, by taking on our mortality, he has conferred his immortality upon us; that, accepting our weakness, he has strengthened us by his power; that, receiving our poverty unto himself, he has transferred his wealth to us; that, taking the weight of our iniquity upon himself (which oppressed us), he has clothed us with his righteousness. (IV.xvii.2; 1362)

Why the Emphasis on Christ's Body and Blood?

It is sometimes said that union with Christ is the heart of Calvin's theology of the Eucharist. Though not false, this is incomplete and misleading. Cal-

---

5. In my essay "John Calvin's Theology of the Eucharist," in *A Companion to the Eucharist in the Reformation,* ed. Lee Palmer Wandel (Leiden: Brill, 2013), I argued that partaking of Christ is, for Calvin, the same as enjoying the benefits of Christ's dwelling within us. I now think that that was a mistake on my part. It has to be said, however, that Calvin was less than fully explicit in distinguishing between our partaking and the benefits thereof, nor was he consistent on the matter. He says in one place, for example, "It is through [the Holy Spirit's] incomprehensible power that we come to partake of Christ's flesh and blood" (*Institutes* IV.xvii.23; p. 1405). I think this comment fits better Christ's working within us, which is the benefit of our partaking, than it does our partaking as such.

vin does sometimes say that a person of faith is united with Christ upon eating the bread and drinking the wine of the Eucharist. But far more often he says that he or she *partakes of the body and blood* of Christ. Reference to Christ's body and blood, for which the bread and the wine stand, is indispensable for Calvin. There are some, he says, who hold that communion with Christ consists of being "partakers of the Spirit only, omitting mention of flesh and blood" (IV.xvii.7; 1367). Calvin rejects this.

A fundamental component of Calvin's Christology, and a fundamental presupposition of his theology of the Eucharist, is that the ascended Christ retains human nature, more specifically, retains a human body — glorified, but still human (IV.xvii.26). The ascension did not mean that Jesus Christ disappeared and that what remained was just the second person of the Trinity. Christ "did not put off the flesh" (IV.xvii.29; 1399). The ascended Christ remains *Jesus* Christ. It was to keep before us that we partake of *the flesh-and-blood Jesus Christ* that Calvin almost always speaks of partaking of the flesh and blood of Christ. "The flesh and blood of Christ" is to be understood as a synecdoche for the flesh-and-blood Jesus Christ. It is of the once-and-still embodied Jesus Christ that we partake.

Calvin has an additional reason for insisting on speaking of partaking of the flesh and blood of Christ. Many of the actions that Christ performs for us and within us are benefits brought about by the shedding of his blood and by his bodily death. So "if the reason for communicating with Jesus Christ is in order that we have part and portion in all the gifts that he has procured for us by his death, it is not only a matter of being partakers of his Spirit; it is necessary also to partake of his humanity, in which he rendered complete obedience to God his Father, to satisfy our debts; though rightly speaking, the one cannot be without the other. For when he gives himself to us, it is in order that we possess him entirely."[6]

Enactment of the Eucharist as Christ Sealing His Promises

Though Calvin says a good deal more about the Eucharist than what I have thus far presented, this is the core of his analysis. The other points he makes either flesh out the analysis or take note of other, more peripheral, dimensions of the eucharistic actions. But before we move on to discuss the understanding of God implicit in the core of his analysis, we should

6. "Short Treatise," pp. 146-47.

take up a point of which Calvin makes a good deal and which became prominent in what the Reformed confessions say about the Eucharist.

Calvin holds that by the presider's action of offering the congregants bread and wine, Christ *seals* (confirms, ratifies) that he really is offering himself to us for our partaking. "That sacred partaking of his flesh and blood, by which Christ pours his life into us, as if it penetrated into our bones and marrow, he also testifies and seals in the Supper — not by presenting a vain and empty sign, but by manifesting there the effectiveness of his Spirit to fulfill what he promises" (IV.xvii.10; 1370).[7]

To fully understand what Calvin has in mind here, we have to bring into the picture his understanding of the ways in which the Eucharist both resembles and differs from Scripture and sermon. The Eucharist is like Scripture and sermon in that, to put it very generally, in both of them Christ offers himself to us: "let it be regarded as a settled principle, that the sacraments have the same office as the Word of God: to offer and set forth Christ to us, and in him the treasures of heavenly grace" (IV.xiv.17; 1292). What's different about the sacraments is that, rather than employing conventional linguistic terms "to offer and set forth Christ to us," they "set before our eyes" what they signify (IV.xiv.10; 1286). They pictorially represent what they signify. The sacramental symbol "truly exhibits" what it symbolizes (IV.xvii.21; 1385). "By the showing of the symbol the thing itself is shown" (IV.xvii.10; 1371). What is shown is that Christ offers himself to us; and that he does so not in some general way but that he offers himself to us *for our partaking of him.*

For us human beings, embodied creatures and often weak in faith, this picturing serves the function of "making it more evident to us" that Christ is indeed offering himself (IV.xiv.3; 1278) and of making more evident to us the nature of Christ's offering. It speaks both to our "dullness" of mind and to our "weakness" of faith (IV.xiv.3; 1278). "As our faith is slight and feeble unless it be propped on all sides and sustained by every means, it trembles, wavers, totters, and at last gives way. Here our merciful Lord, according to his infinite kindness, so tempers himself to our capacity that, since we are creatures who always creep on the ground, cleave to the flesh, and do not think about or even conceive of anything spiritual,

---

7. Cf. Question 75 of the Heidelberg Catechism: "How is it signified and sealed unto you in the holy supper that you partake of the one sacrifice of Christ, accomplished on the cross, and of all his benefits?" And Article 33 of the Belgic Confession: "We believe that our gracious God, taking account of our weakness and infirmities, has ordained the sacraments for us, thereby to seal unto us His promises, and to be pledges of the good will and grace of God towards us, and also to nourish and strengthen our faith."

he condescends to lead us to himself even by these earthly elements, and to set before us in the flesh a mirror of spiritual blessings" (IV.xiv.3; 1278). "The clearer anything is, the fitter it is to support faith. But the sacraments bring the clearest promises; and they have this characteristic over and above the word because they represent them for us as painted in a picture from life" (IV.xiv.5; 1280).

Upon encountering Calvin's idea that by way of the presider's offering bread and wine to the congregants, Christ confirms and seals to them that he is indeed offering himself to them for their partaking, one initially thinks that this confirming or sealing action of Christ is an action in addition to his offering himself. But closer reading of the passages makes quite clear that that is not how Calvin was thinking. The presider's actions do not count as two actions on Christ's part: offering himself for our partaking, and sealing that he is indeed doing so. Rather than being a separate action, sealing is, as it were, an adverbial modifier of the action of offering. By virtue of the pictorial nature and function of the actions performed by the presider, Christ offers himself to us for our partaking *in a sealing or confirming way.*[8]

In the preceding chapter I mentioned that in this chapter I would be making an addition to what I said there about Calvin's analysis of what takes place in the reading of Scripture and the preaching of the sermon. There I argued that, on Calvin's understanding of these, God speaks to us here and now by way of the reading and the preaching; the reading and the preaching count as God saying something to us here and now. I endorsed this Calvinistic interpretation of these liturgical actions.

From Calvin's analysis of the Eucharist, coupled with his comparison of the Eucharist with Scripture reading and preaching, it becomes clear that Calvin holds that something more takes place in Scripture reading and preaching than that, by way of these actions, God here and now says something to us in the form of promise and command, to which the appropriate response is faith and obedience. The "more" that happens is that Christ offers himself to us — offers to dwell within us. Christ does so in the Eucharist as well. His offering of himself in the Eucharist is different, however, in that it is accomplished in a confirmatory sealing manner.

In the Reformed tradition it is rather often said that preaching and the Eucharist are both modes of proclamation, the proclamation being

---

8. In my essay, "John Calvin's Theology of the Eucharist," I took for granted that Calvin understood Christ's sealing or confirming as an action distinct from the action of Christ offering himself for our partaking. I now think that I was mistaken on that point as well.

verbal in preaching and pictorial in the Eucharist; Barth follows in this tradition. If Calvin had said nothing more about the Eucharist than that here God signs and seals his promises, that would be a plausible interpretation of his view. But it should be clear by now that it was far from being Calvin's view that the Eucharist is simply an alternative pictorial mode of proclamation. In the Eucharist, Christ offers himself for our partaking; that is not to be identified with proclaiming Jesus Christ.

Something else happens in the Eucharist that also makes it different from the sermon. For Calvin, the Eucharist is not completed by Christ offering himself to us for our partaking; it is completed only when we actually partake of Christ, when we receive Christ into ourselves, by eating the bread and drinking the wine, whereupon, by the power of the Spirit, Christ then dwells and works within us for our justification, sanctification, and glorification. Our ingesting the bread and wine makes it clear that our reception of Christ's offering is not a matter merely of believing. To repeat a passage quoted above, the life we receive from Christ is not "received by mere knowledge. As it is not the seeing but the eating of bread that suffices to feed the body, so the soul must truly and deeply become partaker of Christ that it may be quickened to spiritual life by his power."

Calvin's teaching concerning partaking of Jesus Christ and the benefits thereof reminds one of the doctrine of divinization *(theosis)* common in Eastern Orthodoxy. Formulations of the doctrine vary somewhat. Some theologians say that divinization consists of becoming God; others say that it consists of becoming like God; yet others say that it consists of partaking of the divine nature.[9] A sentence from Irenaeus is commonly quoted: "If the Word has been made man, it is so that men may be made gods" (*Adv. Haer. V,* Preface). An especially striking statement of this last version of the doctrine is to be found in an unexpected place, namely, C. S. Lewis's *Mere Christianity.* Here is what Lewis says:

> The command *Be ye perfect* is not idealistic gas. Nor is it a command to do the impossible. He is going to make us into creatures that can obey that command. He said (in the Bible) that we were "gods" and He is going to make good His words. If we let Him — for we can prevent Him, if we choose — He will make the feeblest and filthiest of us into a god or god-

---

9. Article 460 of the *Catholic Catechism* (1995) says that "the Word became flesh to make us partakers of the divine nature." For a general discussion of divinization, and for references to the passages quoted, see the Wikipedia article "Divinization (Christian)."

dess, a dazzling, radiant, immortal creature, pulsating all through with such energy and joy and wisdom and love as we cannot now imagine, a bright stainless mirror which reflects back to God perfectly (though, of course, on a smaller scale) His own boundless power and delight and goodness. The process will be long and in parts very painful; but that is what we are in for. Nothing less. He meant what He said.[10]

Though Calvin's teaching unmistakably resembles the various formulations of the doctrine of divinization, it differs from most of them in Calvin's insistence that it is not of the divine nature that we partake in the Eucharist, but of the once-and-still-embodied Jesus Christ.

The Implicit Understanding of God

In our discussion of the Eucharist thus far we have been engaged in the first stage in the formation of liturgical theology, the stage in which we analyze what is going on in some part of the liturgy. But here as elsewhere our analysis has unavoidably overlapped with the second stage, that in which we make explicit the understanding of God implicit in the liturgy. Much of the understanding of God implicit in the Eucharist on Calvin's analysis has already been made explicit. So what I will mainly do in the remainder of this chapter is highlight some of what we have learned and look at it from a number of different angles.

Before doing so, however, I should perhaps say once again that I realize full well that the analysis of the Eucharist that I have presented, namely, Calvin's analysis, is controversial. Some will prefer a traditional Catholic analysis, according to which the high point is the consecration of the elements rather than the offering and the ingesting of bread and wine. A good many Protestants will prefer a Zwinglian analysis, according to which the Eucharist is nothing more than a sacrifice of praise and thanksgiving on our part. This is not the occasion to defend Calvin's analysis against these and other alternatives. And of course there will be yet others who themselves have no view as to what transpires in the Eucharist but find it impossible to give credence to Calvin's "high" view of what takes place. The understanding of God that one regards as implicit in the Eucharist will of course differ depending on how one analyzes what takes place in the Eucharist.

10. C. S. Lewis, *Mere Christianity* (New York: Macmillan, 1954), p. 160.

I have argued that an enactment of the Christian liturgy is the site of mutual address between God and God's people. A point that I have not previously made explicitly is that mutual address, when conducted in a spirit of mutual love, is a form of communion between persons. An enactment of the Christian liturgy is the site of *communion* between God and God's people.

Liturgical communion between God and God's people attains its highest form in the Eucharist. By eating the bread and drinking the wine we receive Christ into ourselves, whereupon Christ dwells and works within us. This is a form of communion that goes far beyond that which takes place in mutual address; indeed, it has no close analogue in human interactions. When we were discussing mutual address between God and the people, we could point to close analogues in how we human beings relate to each other and could use those analogues to illuminate what takes place in the liturgy. The form of communion that takes place in an enactment of the Eucharist has no close analogue in how we human beings relate to each other; the analogue bequeathed to us by Christ himself is that of ingesting bread and wine. The God who is of unsurpassable excellence does not only stoop down to listen to us, to hear us, and to speak to us; God stoops down to dwell and work within us in the person of Jesus Christ through the action of the Holy Spirit. In mutual speaking and listening, there remains a certain distance between the interlocutors; in the communion that takes place in the Eucharist, all distance is removed.

A different but related point is the following. Actions of addressing God are not, as such, Christological in character. Their content may be Christological; often it is. But they are not Christological just by virtue of being instances of addressing God. By contrast, eucharistic actions, on Calvin's analysis, are intrinsically Christological: Christ offers himself for our partaking and we accept the offer. The theology implicit in the Eucharist is intrinsically Christological.

I have already taken note of one aspect of the Christology implicit in the Eucharist on Calvin's analysis: the ascension of Jesus did not represent the second person of the Trinity shucking off human nature, with the consequence that Jesus Christ went out of existence. It is of Jesus Christ that we partake; hence Calvin's insistence on saying that we partake of the *flesh and blood* of Christ.

The aspect of Christology most prominent in Calvin's analysis, however, is that Christ does not just "accomplish" our salvation by his incarnation, crucifixion, resurrection, and ascension, it then being up to us to grab hold by faith of what he has accomplished. By the action of the Holy Spirit Christ dwells and works within us to sanctify us. The Christology implicit in the Eucharist, on Calvin's analysis, is a Christology that comes to expression in the gospel of John and in certain of Paul's letters.

Here is part of what Jesus says in one of his disputes with his antagonists:

> Truly, truly, I say to you, unless you eat the flesh of the Son of man and drink his blood, you have no life in you; he who eats my flesh and drinks my blood has eternal life, and I will raise him up at the last day. For my flesh is food indeed, and my blood is drink indeed. He who eats my flesh and drinks my blood *abides* in me, and I in him. (John 6:53-56; emphasis mine)

Here is part of what Jesus says in his farewell discourse to his disciples:

> He who *abides* in me, and I in him, he it is that bears much fruit, for apart from me you can do nothing. (John 15:5; emphasis mine)

And here is what Paul says in his Letter to the Romans:

> But you are not in the flesh, you are in the Spirit, if in fact the Spirit of God dwells in you. Any one who does not have the Spirit of Christ does not belong to him. But if Christ is *in* you, although your bodies are dead because of sin, your spirits are alive because of doing what is right. (Rom. 8:9-11; emphasis mine)[11]

In the Eucharist, on Calvin's analysis, we enact Johannine and Pauline Christology.

It would be interesting and valuable to see in detail how a Christology (and Pneumatology) that begins from what is implicit in the Eucharist would differ from traditional Christologies. I would guess that by virtue of beginning from Christ's present indwelling in believers, rather than from the events that took place in Bethlehem two millennia ago, it would be significantly different in its configuration. But only if someone actually develops a liturgical Christology can we be sure.

---

11. "Doing what is right" is my translation of the Greek word *dikaiosunē*. The RSV and the NRSV both translate it as "righteousness."

Afterword

To be inducted into the Christian liturgy is to acquire a certain understanding of God — call it, the *liturgical understanding.* Some of that understanding is explicit in the enactment of whatever particular liturgy one participates; much of it is implicit. My project in this volume has been to make explicit some of what is implicit.

Paradoxical

The liturgical understanding of God proves to be strikingly paradoxical. Christians assemble for the enactment of their liturgy in order to worship God. They also expect or hope that they will be built up in their devotion to God, both for their life when assembled and for their life when dispersed; but it is by worshipping God in the way they do that they hope or expect to be built up in devotion.

Worship, in general, is adoration. In each case it acquires its particular contour from the object of adoration and from the worshipper's understanding of that object. I have argued that prominent in the Christian liturgical adoration of God is awed adoration of God for God's inestimably great glory, reverential adoration of God for God's inestimably great holiness, and grateful adoration of God for God's inestimably great love for us, God's human creatures.

It was when we turned to consider the normative status of worshipping God that the paradoxical character of the liturgical understanding of God began to come to light. Worshipping God is not just a good thing for human beings in general, and for the church in particular, to do; it is

163

something we ought to do, something that is due God. Failure to do so is to wrong God. But obviously it is not something that we human beings do inevitably, unavoidably, ineluctably; God has created us free to worship or not to worship God. The fact that we owe it to God to worship God, plus the fact that God created us free to do so or not, implies that God made Godself vulnerable to being wronged by us.

When we look inside the liturgy at the act of confession, we discover that the understanding of God implicit in this liturgical act is not just that God is *vulnerable* to being wronged but that God has *in fact* been wronged; we confess to God the wrong we have done God. And when we look inside the liturgy at our intercessions and our blessing of God, we discover that the understanding of God implicit in these liturgical acts is that God is vulnerable not just to being wronged but to resistance to God's act of bringing about God's kingdom. Of course, our wronging of God is itself resistance to God's bringing about of the kingdom.

This is highly paradoxical: that the God of inestimable excellence in glory, holiness, and love would allow Godself to be vulnerable to being wronged and to being resisted. But paradox goes deeper yet.

The most prominent acts in the liturgy, when viewed from the side of the people, are the congregants speaking and the congregants listening. A good number of liturgical acts are of neither of these two types — dropping one's offering in a basket, for example. Nonetheless, the two types of acts most prominent in the liturgy are those that consist of the congregants speaking and those that consist of the congregants listening.

Most speaking by the congregants consists of their addressing God in the expectation that God will listen and in the expectation or hope that God will hear favorably. And I have argued that most listening by the congregants is to be understood as their listening to what God is saying to them by way of the speech of some human being. Enactment of the liturgy is the site of mutual address and listening between God and the people.

When we reflect on the normative implications of this mutual address and listening, the conclusion to which we are led is that God humbles Godself to listen and speak to us and simultaneously elevates us by inviting us to speak to God and by authorizing a mere human being to speak on God's behalf. Amazing paradox: that the God of inestimable greatness in glory, holiness, and love would humble Godself and elevate us so that we can engage in mutual address and listening. What we learned when we explored the Eucharist is that the God of inestimable greatness and excellence not only listens and speaks to us but, in Jesus Christ, humbles

Godself by offering to dwell and work within us for our sanctification. Amazing paradox!

Why Do Liturgical Theology?

In my opening chapter I raised the question, why do liturgical theology? What's the point? Why not be content with the other types of theology on offer? I said that I would postpone answering the question until we had some actual liturgical theology in hand. Now we do. So it's time to offer an answer.

In its practice of interpreting and applying the Bible the church hands on its understanding of God as presented in Scripture. In its practice of reciting and teaching its creeds, confessions, and catechisms the church hands on what it has officially declared that it believes about God. In its practice of enacting the liturgy the church hands on the understanding of God implicit in its worship. These are three distinct but interacting dimensions of the tradition of the church.

These three dimensions of the church's tradition do not exhaust what the church hands on. The church also hands on how it serves and obeys God in its life in the everyday; this too is a dimension of its tradition. But for our purpose here of explaining the importance of liturgical theology, nothing will be lost if we set this additional aspect of the church's tradition off to the side, important though it is.

We who are Christians are inducted into all three dimensions, thereby being formed and disciplined by all three: inducted into the church's tradition of Scripture interpretation, inducted into the tradition of the church's declaration of what it believes, inducted into the tradition of Christian liturgy. By virtue of our induction, each dimension works on us in its own distinctive way. Of course, with respect to the first and the third we are not just inducted into the tradition as such, but into some particular version of the tradition. And with respect to the second, we are not just inducted into what the church universal declares it believes but into some particular confessional tradition. The tradition of the church, in its threefold form, is like traditions in general in that it incorporates disagreement and controversy.

The tradition of the church, in its threefold form, is also like traditions in general in that it carries authority for those who are inducted into the tradition. The distinct character of the authority of the first two dimensions of the tradition of the church has been discussed often and at length;

the distinct character of the authority of the liturgical dimension of the church's tradition has been discussed less, and hardly at all by Protestants.

An apothegm coming down to us from the Church Fathers is *lex orandi, lex credendi*. The saying is cryptic and susceptible to different interpretations. It would be of some interest to survey the different ways in which theologians have interpreted and employed the saying. Here let me just note that the saying can be interpreted as a crisp way of stating what I have just now said, namely, that the liturgical tradition of the church has authority.

Without undertaking here to characterize that authority, let me repeat what I said earlier, namely, that I see it as rooted in the fact that the traditional liturgies have stood the test of time by massive numbers of Christians. Over almost two millennia members of the church around the globe have assembled each Sunday to enact one or another of these liturgies. If at some point there were something seriously mistaken in their implicit or explicit understanding of God, it is enormously likely that that part of the liturgy would long ago have been rejected; Christian worshippers would have felt in their bones that it had to go.

Corresponding to each of the three dimensions of the church's tradition, the scriptural, the conciliar-creedal, and the liturgical, there is a certain kind of theology. Corresponding to the first dimension of the church's tradition is the articulation by theologians, on behalf of the church, of the understanding of God explicit and implicit in Scripture as interpreted by the church. Corresponding to the second dimension is the articulation by theologians, on behalf of the church, of the understanding of God explicit and implicit in the conciliar and creedal declarations of the church. Corresponding to the third dimension is the articulation by theologians, on behalf of the church, of the understanding of God explicit and implicit in its liturgy. The first of these is biblical theology; the second might be called conciliar-creedal theology; the third is liturgical theology.

The church has a rich heritage of biblical theology and of conciliar-creedal theology; it is evident to all that each of these has its own distinct character. If liturgical theology turned out not to be significantly different from one or the other of these, that would be a reason for not bothering with it. With a sample of liturgical theology now in hand, I trust that no reader will doubt that liturgical theology is significantly different from both biblical and conciliar-creedal theology. Liturgical theology does not contradict those other forms of theology; at many points, it overlaps them. But it has its own distinct configuration. Much of what it highlights, the others place in the shadows. Liturgical theology highlights God as listener and God as vulnerable. Conciliar-creedal theology says nothing about either of these.

One might ask why it is that these three forms of theology turn out significantly different from each other. The answer, surely, is that it's because they focus on three significantly different aspects of the tradition of the church: the church's practice of interpreting Scripture is significantly different from the church's practice of formulating and teaching creeds, confessions, and catechisms; and both of those are significantly different, in turn, from the church's practice of assembling to enact its liturgy. The understandings of God implicit and explicit in these practices are different because the practices are different.

So once again: why do liturgical theology? For the same reason that theologians of the church have developed biblical theology and conciliar-creedal theology. All three of these articulate, and when called for, critique, the understanding of God that the church hands on: biblical theology articulates the church's understanding of the biblical presentation of God and critiques that understanding when it sees critique as called for; conciliar-creedal theology articulates the church's conciliar and creedal understanding of God and critiques that understanding when it sees critique as called for; liturgical theology articulates the church's liturgical understanding of God and critiques that understanding when it sees critique as called for.

Let's call the three types of theology that we have just now identified, *church-reflexive theology,* the idea being that here the church articulates and critiques the understanding of God implicit and explicit in its own threefold tradition. What is commonly called *constructive* theology is distinct from church-reflexive theology. The constructive theologian articulates his or her own views about God. If she is a Christian theologian, Christian Scripture and the conciliar and creedal declarations of the church carry considerable weight for her; my view is that the liturgy should do so as well. But the project of the constructive theologian is not to articulate the theology implicit and explicit in the church's threefold tradition but to develop his or her own thoughts about God.

Constructive theology in the West has been powerfully shaped by the concern that it measure up to the requirements for being a respectable academic discipline. Given Aquinas's Aristotelian mentality, it comes as no surprise to discover that he was concerned, in *Summa Theologiae,* to establish that theology is a genuine *scientia.* To this present author it did come as a surprise to discover that one of Karl Barth's concerns, in the Prolegomena to his *Church Dogmatics,* was to establish that theology is a genuine *Wissenschaft.*[1]

A variant of the concern of the constructive theologian that theology measure up to the requirements for being a genuine *scientia* or *Wissenschaft* is the concern that it have, and be shown to have, secure epistemological warrant for the claims it makes about God. What else would account for the fact that the prolegomena of so many constructive theologies is a discourse on revelation, and more generally, on how we know God? Even Calvin, who said that his project in the *Institutes* was to cultivate piety in his readers by offering them guidance on how to interpret Scripture, opens with a lengthy discourse on how we know God. The liturgical theologian would not think of beginning in this way. We who participate in enacting the liturgy do so on the assumption that we know enough about God to worship God in the way Christians do.

Yet another type of theology is what one might call *formation* theology, by which I mean, theology aimed at exercising a formative influence on the thought or life of the church. Calvin's theology in the *Institutes,* at least as he himself described it, was formation theology; he aimed at forming the piety of his readers. The theology of St. Benedict, as described in the wonderful book by Jean Leclercq, *The Love of Learning and the Desire for God,* was formation theology, aimed at shaping the life of the monastic community of which Benedict was the leader.[2]

A Challenge to Traditional Philosophical Theology

The liturgical theology that has emerged in the course of our discussion poses a challenge to a good deal of traditional philosophical theology. Traditional philosophical theology begins by asking what God has to be like given the way the world is; it adds to this the thesis that God is perfect — a being than which there can be none greater or more excellent. It concludes that God is pure act *(actus purus),* eternal, unconditioned, immutable, and so forth.

Liturgical theology highlights the fact that God listens to what we say

1. See the opening section of Barth's *Church Dogmatics.*
2. Jean Leclercq, *The Love of Learning and the Desire for God: A Study of Monastic Culture* (New York: Fordham University Press, 1982).

to God. It would seem that God's listening to what we say to God occurs when we say it. If so, that appears to conflict with the claim that God is eternal, outside of time. It also appears to conflict with the claim that God is immutable. If God listens to what we say to God when we say it, that would seem to constitute a change in God — just as there is a change in my life when I listen to what you say to me. And if God's listening to what we say to God does indeed constitute a change in God's life, then it would seem that we have to give up the doctrine of divine aseity or unconditionedness; God's listening to what we say to God has a condition outside of God, namely, our saying something to God. God is not pure act.

These quick comments fall far short of establishing incompatibility between liturgical theology and the traditional doctrines of divine eternity, immutability, and aseity; to actually establish incompatibility, assuming it can be established, would require a great deal of hard, careful work. And if incompatibility can be established, it is always open to the philosophical theologian either to dismiss the liturgy as misguided in what it assumes about God, or to follow in the footsteps of Maimonides by arguing that the theology I have claimed to be implicit in the liturgy is not in fact implicit and to offer an alternative Maimonides-style analysis according to which there is no incompatibility between the conclusions of philosophical theology and what is implicit in the liturgy.

Whatever the outcome of such discussions, the liturgical theology that has emerged from our discussion does at least pose a challenge to traditional philosophical theology, a challenge that, to the best of my knowledge, none of those who have written about philosophical theology has taken into account — I include myself in this generalization. I now regard that as a serious shortcoming.

In Conclusion

Of the various forms of theology mentioned above, liturgical theology is probably "the least of these." But it does have a tradition; it did not begin with this present book. I have mentioned Alexander Schmemann and J.-J. von Allmen as two revered predecessors; I could name others.

That said, those familiar with the tradition of liturgical theology will find my contribution to the tradition highly idiosyncratic. Whereas I have devoted several chapters to the liturgical understanding of God as one who listens and hears, no other liturgical theologian, to the best of my knowledge, has discussed this aspect of what God does. Nor, to the best of my knowledge, has any other liturgical theologian discussed the liturgical understanding of God as one who is vulnerable to being wronged and being resisted.

Why is the liturgical theology that I have developed and presented so different from that of others? Part of the answer is that, as every reader will have realized, my training and expertise are those of a philosopher whereas the training and expertise of Schmemann, von Allmen, and their colleagues are those of theologians. That difference is bound to yield a significant difference in results.

But that cannot be the entire explanation. There is nothing in the training and expertise of theologians that prevents them from discussing God as listener and hearer. Something else is at work causing the difference. What might that be?

I think part of the answer is the following. I quoted Schmemann as saying that the goal of liturgical theology is to uncover the theological "logos" of the liturgy, its theological "meaning." The liturgy, he says, contains theology "in code"; the task of the liturgical theologian is to "decode" the code. I interpreted Schmemann as meaning that the task of the liturgical theologian is to make explicit and articulate the understanding of God implicit in the liturgy. That is what I have done.

But when one actually looks at what Schmemann does, I think most of it is better described as *theological reflections about* liturgy than as *making explicit and articulating the theology implicit in* the liturgy. The same is true for all the other liturgical theology with which I am familiar, including von Allmen's: it is theology *of* liturgy. Naturally there will be cases on the borderline between theology of liturgy and making explicit the theology implicit in liturgy. But I submit that most liturgical theology fits much better under the former concept than under the latter. The opposite is true for most of my discussion.

Is this the entire answer to the question why this present book has turned out to be so different from other liturgical theology? Could it be that part of the reason liturgical theologians have not discussed God as listener and God as vulnerable is that they too have been influenced by the long tradition of thinking of God as pure act, *actus purus?* Listening is an act, of course. But it is not "pure" act. It is response.

Subject Index

God, 128-30, 139; on the nature and purpose of the church to enact the liturgy, 11-12; and the ontology of the liturgy, 9-12; on prophetic proclamation of the Word, 64-65, 127, 129-30; on three ways God addresses us in the liturgy, 65-66, 127

White, Roger M., 91
Woolfe, Zachary, 92
Worship: in acts of confession and intercession, 38-39; in acts of listening, 38-39; adoration, 25-26, 38, 163; amazement/awe, 26, 28-33, 52, 163; attitudinal stance, 24-26, 38, 163; definition and distinctiveness of, 23-26, 38; Godward orientation that characterizes, 24, 40; gratitude, 26, 37, 163; relation of proclamation to, 38-39; reverence, 26, 33-37, 163. *See also* God as worthy of worship
Worship: Its Theology and Practice (von Allmen), 9-10
Wright, N. T.: contrasted to Barth, 130-31; on early Christian kingdom-language, 122; on first-century Jewish exorcisms, 121; on Paul's messianic language, 122-23; on what Jesus meant by the coming kingdom of God, 113-23

Scripture Index